CW00348697

TURNER CLASSIC MOVIES BF

The Tauris British Film Guide series has, tributed to the revaluation of British cine British films from the past hundred years. I.B.Tauris has now entered an exciting and innovative partnership with TCM (Turner Classic Movies), the premier movie channel dedicated to keeping the classic movies alive for fans old and new. With a striking new design and new identity, the series will continue to provide what the *Guardian* has called 'a valuable resource of critical work on the UK's neglected film history'. Each film guide will establish the historical and cinematic context of the film, provide a detailed critical reading and assess the reception and after-life of the production. The series will continue to draw on all genres and all eras, building over time into a wide-ranging library of informed, in-depth books on the films that will comprehensively refute the ill-informed judgement of French director François Truffaut that there was a certain incompatibility between the terms British and cinema. It will demonstrate the variety, creativity, humanity, poetry and mythic power of the best of British cinema in volumes designed to be accessible to film enthusiasts, scholars and students alike.

TCM is the definitive classic movie channel available on cable, satellite and digital terrestrial TV <www.tcmonline.co.uk>.

JEFFREY RICHARDS
General Editor

British Film Guides published and forthcoming:

Whiskey Galore! and The Maggie Colin McArthur
The Charge of the Light Brigade Mark Connelly
Get Carter Steve Chibnall
Dracula Peter Hutchings
The Private Life of Henry VIII Greg Walker
My Beautiful Laundrette Christine Geraghty
Brighton Rock Steve Chibnall
A Hard Day's Night Stephen Glynn
If Paul Sutton
Black Narcissus Sarah Street
The Red Shoes Mark Connelly
Saturday Night and Sunday Morning Anthony Aldgate
A Clockwork Orange I.Q.Hunter
Four Weddings and a Funeral Andrew Spicer

TURNER CLASSIC MOVIE BRITISH FILM GUIDE

My Beautiful Laundrette

CHRISTINE GERAGHTY

I.B. TAURIS

LONDON · NEW YORK

Published in 2005 by I.B.Tauris & Co. Ltd
6 Salem Road, London W2 4BU
175 Fifth Avenue, New York NY 10010
www.ibtauris.com

In the United States of America and Canada distributed by Palgrave Macmillan,
a division of St Martin's Press, 175 Fifth Avenue, New York NY 10010

ISBN   1 85043 414 X
EAN   978 85043 414 6

A full CIP record for this book is available from the British Library
A full CIP record for this book is available from the Library of Congress

Library of Congress catalog card: available

Set in Monotype Fournier and Univers Black by Ewan Smith, London
Printed and bound in Great Britain by TJ International Ltd, Padstow, Cornwall

Contents

Illustrations

These illustrations are used for purposes of critical analysis.

Acknowledgements

Many people have discussed *My Beautiful Laundrette* with me and I am grateful to them for their help and tolerance. In particular, I would like to thank Andy Graham, Andy Medhurst, Duncan Petrie, Roy Stafford and Parminder Vir for help with specific points and, more generally, Richard Smith who assisted with bibliographical research; any errors, though, are entirely mine. Ideas were tested out in papers given to the British Cinema History group at the University of London, at Sussex and Glasgow Universities and at the British Film Institute Film and Media Summer School, all of which generated helpful and interesting comments. I particularly thank Henry Bacon for inviting me to speak at the British Cinema Seminar he arranged through the Finnish Film Archive and the University of Helsinki in April 2002, and would also like to thank the British Council for its financial support for that event. On a personal level, I am as always grateful to Paul Marks for his love and support.

This book was completed while on study leave from Goldsmiths College, University of London, and I am very grateful to the college for that generous help. I would like also to thank particularly the first-year students on my film and television course at the college who, every year, responded to the opportunity to write about films with enthusiasm and passion. They reminded me, very tolerantly, that *My Beautiful Laundrette* is now an 'old' film. I hope this book will demonstrate why it remains an enjoyable and important one.

Film Credits

MY BEAUTIFUL LAUNDRETTE

Production Company	Working Title/SAF Productions, for Channel 4
Distributors	UK: Mainline; USA: Orion
Director	Stephen Frears
Producers	Sarah Radclyffe and Tim Bevan
Screenplay	Hanif Kureishi
Music Producers	Stanley Myers, Hans Zimmer
Music	Ludus Tonalis
Director of Photography	Oliver Stapleton
Editor	Mick Audsley
Designer	Hugo Luczyc Wyhowski
Sound Recordist	Albert Bailey
Casting	Debbie McWilliams
First Assistant Director	Simon Hinckley
Second Assistant Director	Waldo Roeg
First Assistant Editor	Jason Adams
Second Assistant Editor	Chris Cook
Production Manager	Jane Frazer
Location Manager	Rebecca O'Brien
Dubbing Editor	'Budge' Tremlett
Continuity	Penelope Eyles
Costume Design	Lindy Hemming
Wardrobe Mistress	Karen Sharpe
Make-up	Elaine Carew
Titles	Mainline
Length	3,507 ft
Running Time	97 minutes
UK Première	15 November 1985
US Première	7 March 1986

CAST

Gordon Warnecke	Omar
Daniel Day-Lewis	Johnny
Saeed Jaffrey	Nasser
Roshan Seth	Papa
Shirley Anne Field	Rachel
Rita Wolf	Tania
Derrick Branche	Salim
Souad Faress	Cherry
Charu Bala Chokshi	Bilquis
Persis Maravala	Nasser's Elder Daughter
Nisha Kapur	Nasser's Younger Daughter
Gurdial Sira	Zaki
Shelia Chitnis	Zaki's wife
Neil Cunningham	Englishman
Walter Donohue	Dick O'Donnell
Richard Graham	Genghis
Stephen Marcus	Moose
Dawn Archibald	First Gang Member
Jonathan Moore	Second Gang Member
Winston Graham	First Jamaican
Dudley Thomas	Second Jamaican
Ram John Holder	Poet
Bhasker	Tariq
Ayub Khan Din	Student
Garry Cooper	Squatter
Gerard Horan	Telephone Man
Colin Campbell	'Madame Butterfly' Man
Chris Pitt	First Kid
Kerryann White	Second Kid
Dulice Leicier	Girl in Disco
Badi Uzzaman	Dealer

Introduction

This is a book about a film, *My Beautiful Laundrette*. The traditional
format for such a study is to divide it up into sections on production, film analysis and critical reception. Often this is effective but,
as I worked on *My Beautiful Laundrette*, I felt that a slightly different
format was required. The production/analysis/reception model implies
that it is the production process which produces the film, which is itself
then analysed in detail before turning to an analysis of its audience.
But the film *My Beautiful Laundrette* is not just 97 minutes of 16mm
celluloid produced in the eighteen months or so between commission
and première. The definition of production needs to be extended to
include both the processes of criticism and distribution which make it
a film that people might want and are able to see, and the processes of
debate that fit it into a cultural context and make it 'important' to have
seen it. This process whereby a film is defined to fit certain audiences
and contexts was particularly important for *My Beautiful Laundrette*
as I show in Chapter 1 of the book, which examines how the film was
positioned in the period 1985–88 and how it became that cluster of
images, sounds, debates and commentary which we now know as *My
Beautiful Laundrette*.

Despite this emphasis on the context, I still maintain that it is
what we see on the screen which, in the end, has the power to move,
challenge and inform audiences. So the second chapter of the book is
devoted to a textual study of the film. Critical work on *My Beautiful
Laundrette* has tended to emphasise its social and political importance
but here I concentrate on its aesthetic aspects to indicate how the film
works as cinema and indeed resolves its political tensions through the
magic of cinema.

In the third chapter, I return to wider contexts but this time to
examine the way in which *My Beautiful Laundrette* has remained an
important and watchable film in the 1990s and early 2000s. After the
definition work discussed in Chapter 1, we can see this as a process
of opening out the film again to different uses, through the practices

of list-making. Literary theory has traditionally developed canons of good work that keep novels and plays alive as important measures of standards or pleasures. But we can expand this into a broader notion of lists which includes the canon of good (British) films to which *My Beautiful Laundrette* belongs, but also encompasses other kinds of lists – video and DVD catalogues, museum catalogues, archive collections, official lists, cult lists, exam syllabuses and textbooks, website favourites, filmographies in academic studies, biographies of those who made it. Such lists (using the term in the widest sense) create new audiences for a film, and the more lists it is on the better its chances of maintaining a continuing existence as a film that people, at all sorts of levels, encourage others to see and resee. Chapter 3 indicates how this process has worked for *My Beautiful Laundrette*, and, of course, this book, in a series of British Film Guides, continues the process by adding it to yet another list.

One final word about authorship. *My Beautiful Laundrette* was a significant film for those involved in the making of it, particularly Stephen Frears, the director, and Hanif Kureishi, the writer. It was, in many ways, a starting point for both of them and the film is often discussed in terms of their artistic or personal biographies. They feature in these pages through the interviews they have given in which they make perceptive comments that contribute to how the film is defined and used. But, because of the approach outlined above, I have not sought out their retrospective views. As film-makers they were clearly crucial and we would not have the film without them but, in this short study, I have preferred to let the film float a little freer of authorial intentions than usual, and to retain my emphasis on the role of a wider cultural formation.

ONE
Crossing Over: The Making
of the Film

The term 'cross-over' is consistently used to describe *My Beautiful Laundrette* and in this section I want to look at the making of the film through a number of cross-overs. This will allow us to see how it came to be positioned in a number of key debates and indicate how it also came to be, within less than three years, not only one of Channel 4's biggest commercial successes but also a landmark in critical thinking about representation and cultural diversity. The unlikely story of Omar (Gordon Warnecke) who seeks business success in a run-down launderette and, in the process, falls in love with the brooding Johnny (Daniel Day-Lewis), thus became a film described by Stuart Hall (then Professor of Sociology at the Open University) as 'one of the most riveting and important films produced by a black writer in recent years'.[1]

This section positions *My Beautiful Laundrette* as a cross-over film in a number of ways: in terms of crossing over between television and cinema; as a film that was praised for crossing over from specialist, independent film-making to appeal to popular audiences; as a cross-over film poised between realism and fantasy; and as a film that literally takes crossing over and hybridity as its subject matter. Approaching the film in this way allows us to look at the use made of the film in a specific critical context as well as at elements of production, exhibition and reception which became an integral part of its early history. Readers who prefer to read an analysis of the film first may of course turn to Chapter 2.

FROM TELEVISION TO CINEMA

My Beautiful Laundrette was a Film on Four production, commissioned by the new Channel 4, which began broadcasting in 1982. It was a commercial channel but had a clear public service remit 'to encourage innovation and experiment in the form and content of programmes'.[2] The new channel would, its first chief executive, Jeremy Isaacs, claimed, put 'emphasis on film as an art form and information carrier' in a new way for television and 'glory in the best that was alive and kicking in world cinema'.[3] Film on Four was the production arm established to fulfil part of this remit alongside The Eleventh Hour, which commissioned more experimental work. Cinematic release for television work was a crucial issue since, while putting films on television was a familiar practice, screening films made for television in cinemas was much less so. Up until this point, as Michael Grade polemically put it when chief executive of Channel 4, feature films on the BBC were called plays, shot on 16mm and subject to industrial agreements that inhibited cinematic screenings; Grade looked back on Channel 4 as 'the first broadcaster to create a bridge across the great media divide'.[4] The political economy of the changing relationship between film and television in the 1980s has been well described by John Hill who emphasises, in particular, British cinema's increasing dependence on television for finance and the shift from in-house production to commissioning from independent producers which was the model for the new channel. Hill judges that Channel 4 quickly established itself as 'the most consistent and committed of the television companies involved in film production'.[5] John Pym describes how Channel 4's policy aimed to use cinema exhibition to give a film 'a reputation and an identity' before its two television screenings in the Film on Four slot.[6]

Now that we are so used to the interaction of film, television and video, it is perhaps worth remembering that Channel 4's pronounced diversification into film in the early eighties was controversial, and the debate was the more pointed since cinema admissions dropped from 101 million in 1980 to a low of 54 million in 1984.[7] The debate was not just about whether television could be blamed for this decline but about the essential nature of what could be produced for the cinema and television, about aesthetics, subjects and audience response; for many in the film industry, the films made for Film on Four (and the BBC) represented a threat to the essence of cinema. The British Film Institute's critical magazine, *Sight & Sound*, published a number of such debates in the early eighties, and its pages reverberated to the sound of axes being ground. Film producer Simon Perry, commenting in 1981 from Cannes on the growing importance of television sales for films, provides a typical assertion of the binary opposition on which fears were built:

Artistically, television values are different from cinema values. The small screen can really only convey one piece of visual information at a time, preferably one which occupies a substantial area of the frame; complex compositions tend to befuddle the watcher's eye. To sustain its impact, television is best used as a reportage medium, supplying single strong images in a sequence that equates with verbal exposition.[8]

Channel 4's launch in 1982 did not stem the discussion. In a debate entitled 'British Cinema Life before Death on Television' in spring 1984, the editor of *Sight & Sound*, Penelope Houston, agreed that 'there are crucial aesthetic differences, as well as differences in the quality of the experience',[9] while Mamoun Hassan (then managing director of the National Film Finance Corporation) argued that 'the two media are tuned to different harmonics', television being best for 'explaining and describing' while cinema 'concerns itself with the ineffable, with that which cannot be expressed' (p. 116). The sense, expressed by producer David Puttnam, that films made for television would involve 'a tragic lowering of creative horizons' (p. 117) was strong, the problem lying not only in the small, poor-quality image but also in conditions of viewing, the difference, according to Hassan, between the 'abstract dark of the cinema ... where a crackling piece of paper is an unendurable invasion' and the home in which the interruption of 'a ringing telephone, children, cats, dogs, passing traffic and interruption by commercials can be tolerated and accepted' (p. 116). Such conditions, it was argued, would inevitably mean that form and content had to be adjusted to fit them.

Even those more sympathetic to television in these debates accepted the notion of the essential natures of the different media. Television viewing was associated with smallness, with intimacy. Alan Bennett, a playwright acclaimed for his work for the medium, suggested that for television 'you don't need to raise your voice' (p. 121), while Mark Le Fanu, looking 'Forward into British Film Year', suggested that television should play to its strengths, its capacity for 'a wonderful, quiet knowledge about the intricacies of human motivation'.[10] Given the lack of archiving and critical attention, Bennett rather despairingly concluded that a BBC television film was also ephemeral; it 'has no history', a television play was 'an incident', discussed the next day then gone (p. 121).

Throughout the debate, cinema is seen as the place where cultural value can be conferred despite or perhaps because of the bigger, but distracted, audiences provided by television. For those most firmly in the cinema lobby, television seemed to be looking to cinema to 'stand the cost of a lavish launch'.[11] There was a tendency also for film-makers to feel that Channel 4 was not allowing enough time to build up the film's cinematic value before it was undermined by a television screening. This problem was made worse in the early years because of the need for programmes to fill the new channel's schedule and the Cinematograph Exhibitors Association's ruling that films that would be on television within three years should not be screened theatrically; certainly, Channel 4 was felt to have denied or severely curtailed the theatrical life of films such as *The Ploughman's Lunch* (1983) or *The Draughtsman's Contract* (1982).[12]

This ongoing debate provides the background against which to examine what it meant for *My Beautiful Laundrette* to cross over from television to cinema in terms of the framework of cultural value and audience address which was involved. *Laundrette* was intended by David Rose as 'a modest film for television'.[13] Kureishi's script was set in contemporary London and focused on Omar, a British Pakistani who is given a run-down launderette as a business opportunity by his Uncle Nasser (Saeed Jaffrey). Omar seeks the help of Johnny, a former friend, now part of a racist gang. Despite Nasser's hopes that Omar will marry his daughter Tania (Rita Wolf), the two young men become lovers as they transform the launderette. In the end, Johnny chooses to stand by Omar and fights off the gang's attack on the launderette. The small budget of around £600,000 was provided by Channel 4, which fully funded the project. As Working Title producer Tim Bevan told *Screen International*, this took the pressure off selling the film because 'we haven't had to have a completion guarantee'. What was described as 'a television film' completed its shoot, in 16mm, on location in Stockwell and Kingston in April 1985, and was scheduled for a television slot in November that year.[14]

The director, Stephen Frears, was known as someone whose con-siderable skills had largely been gained in directing television plays at the BBC, an experience he later looked back on with pleasure; 'for a long time', he said of his working practices in 1970s television, 'I made films for people who only wanted them to be as good as pos-sible'.[15] Frears had directed his first feature film, *Gumshoe*, in 1971 but had then consistently worked in television, relishing the opportunity for collaborative work and welcoming British television's embrace of the 'concept of social realism, not at a particularly ferocious level, but simply by giving an accurate account of what it's like to live in Britain'.[16] Frears even welcomed television's notorious ephemerality; 'I could actually make a case for things being ephemeral,' he said in an interview at the time of the release of *My Beautiful Laundrette*, 'the idea of making something to last is appalling.' He added that the film's theatrical release did not change his view that it could only have been made for television. It would not have been 'a commercial proposition', the story would have been impossible to pitch and a larger budget would have weighed the film down.[17] *My Beautiful Laundrette* was not Frears's first Film on Four; he had directed *Walter* (1982), which launched the first season on Channel 4's first day of transmission, and followed it up with *Walter and June* (1983).

Hanif Kureishi, who wrote the screenplay, may not have been as familiar with television as Frears but was attracted to it. A promising playwright, with successes at the Royal Court and the Royal Shakespeare Company's experimental Warehouse venue,[18] he described his willingness to take on the commission offered by Karin Banborough from Channel 4 in terms of his interest in the medium and particularly its audience. *Screen International* quoted him as praising the new channel for 'making films for adults – in the tradition of political writing I go back to – and creating a wider intelligent audience'.[19] In the London listing magazine *Time Out*, at the time of the UK release, Kureishi recalled that he had been 'very keen' to write for Film on Four because it had 'taken over from the BBC's "Play for Today" in presenting serious drama about our unhappy democracy to a wide audience'. He cites Bennett, Dennis Potter, Alan Plater and David Mercer as television writers who inspired this ambition and describes how, when he was young, he would 'sit in the train listening to people discussing the previous night's drama and interrupt them with my own opinion'.[20] Kureishi thus gave a positive account of television drama, drawing on his own engagement with it as a viewer to re-create Bennett's lost history of television successes and as evidence of its wide appeal to contemporary audiences. Later on, in the introduction to the screenplay of *My Beautiful Laundrette* published in 1986, Kureishi glosses this matching of subject and audience with a more considered statement: 'the great advantage of TV drama was that people watched it; difficult, challenging things could be said about contemporary life'.[21]

In terms, then, of the commission, the small budget, the use of 16mm film, the director's track record and the ambitions of the scriptwriter, *My Beautiful Laundrette* can be understood as a work for television.

But it crossed over and on 15 November 1985 the film had its first commercial screening, not as planned on television but in the cinema. It is interesting, in this context, to trace how Kureishi's accounts, in the publicity he generated for the film, shift the emphasis from television to cinema at around the time of the film's cinema release. In the *Time Out* article, Kureishi follows his praise of 'Play for Today' with a single-sentence paragraph in which he recalls his decision to take Channel 4's commission – 'So I would do a British film for British Film Year'[22] – thus retrospectively and rather ironically allying his film with British cinema's drive to attract audiences away from television. In an interview for the British Film Institute's *Monthly Film Bulletin*, also published in November 1985, Kureishi again refers to 'the Play for Today tradition', but this time, in a film magazine, goes on to make a connection with cinema. He suggests that British film-makers could learn from that television tradition and seeks to be part of that process; 'it should be the same in the movies: contemporary independent film should be dealing with what life is like in Britain today', he says, adding of *Laundrette*, 'I wanted to do something hard'. In *Monthly Film Bulletin*, also, Kureishi describes his screenplay's origins rather differently. Rather than crediting Banborough's approach as the starting point, he turns to a cinematic tradition, telling how the screenplay started off 'as an idea for something big like *The Godfather*', tracing the progress of a family migrating to Britain in 1945, although film critic Derek Malcolm reported him discussing this as 'what he would now like to write'.[23] In the introduction to the published screenplay, after the film's successful theatrical release, Kureishi further emphasises the wide range of his cinematic ambitions; along with an expanded description of the abandoned parallels with *The Godfather*, he describes how *My Beautiful Laundrette* was 'to have gangster and thriller elements, since the gangster film is the form that corresponds most closely to the city', but the genre mix was also to include irony and comedy, for the film 'was to be an amusement' too. This later version does not, as the *Time Out* article did, state that *My Beautiful Laundrette* was originally intended for television only. Instead, we get the bland sentence 'The film played in the Edinburgh Film Festival and then went into the cinema.'[24]

I am not suggesting that anything is being hidden here, merely that the articles in *Time Out* and *Monthly Film Bulletin*, along with numerous other interviews, were part of the crossing-over process, and that the screenplay introduction appeared after that process had been successfully completed. It therefore plays down the significance of the screening in Edinburgh which Kureishi had dwelt on at length in the earlier version:

> *My Beautiful Laundrette* was originally intended for television only, and it was shot in 16 mm as a TV film. But in September [*sic*] it played the Edinburgh Film Festival and received favourable reviews. People urged us to allow it to be shown in the cinema, arguing that although initially it would be seen by less people, it would receive wider critical coverage and not merely the usual facetious lines that is called television reviewing in this country. We finally agreed to a cinema release.[25]

Here, then, is the mythic turning point and perhaps the decision did not quite need the urging that Kureishi implies.

Certainly the question of a theatrical release was an issue when the film was shown in the festival. Jane Root's programme notes, written before the film had found an audience, seem to accept its television status, making comparisons with two contemporary TV series and offering 'three cheers to Channel 4' for its financing.[26] The critics picked it up not just as 'one of the best Channel 4 films in years' but as a 'British winner'[27] which should be watched out for not on television but in the cinema at the London Film Festival that autumn. A number of critics urged Channel 4 to make it more generally available in cinemas. Derek Malcolm was the most explicit, declaring that *My Beautiful Laundrette* was more than 'merely a good television film' and seeing it as precisely the kind of work that might improve collaboration between the two formats: 'if this ground-breaking, extraordinarily intriguing and undoubtedly controversial production does not reach at least some of this country's cinemas, there isn't really a deal of hope for any effective collaboration between the small screen and the large'.[28] Others joined in. Pam Cook urged: 'Step forward a theatrical distributor', while Iain Johnstone thought Channel 4 'would be prudent to put it in the cinema too'.[29] The large television audiences weighed less here than the impact of cinema in a narrower cultural market. It was a two-way process; cinematic release was considered a reward for the film's worth but the 'buzz of genuine excitement and surprise' it had created was something, Malcolm argued, that British cinema needed.[30]

My Beautiful Laundrette thus received a cinema release. We shall look at its reception and exhibition pattern shortly, but one further point needs to be made when considering the complex relationship between television and cinema. British television has traditionally been seen as a writers' medium, so that authorship provides an explanatory framework

1. *Hanif Kureishi at a party on the set. His authorship was a strong element in publicity for the film.* (*Source*: BFI Collections, courtesy of FilmFour)

for work as different as *Blue Remembered Hills* (Potter, 1979), *Boys from the Blackstuff* (Bleasdale, 1982) and *Prime Suspect* (La Plante, 1991). Kureishi himself indicated this in his list of the television writers he admired, and the *My Beautiful Laundrette* project began, in television's typical manner, with a script commission to a writer. Kureishi describes himself as having a major influence in the choice of director and actors and being 'on hand' throughout the shoot; so involved was he that he sees himself as partly responsible for the set ('we built the launderette ... ') as well as for the final cut ('we then cut forty five minutes out').[31] That the publicity and reviews which accompanied the theatrical release largely focus on Kureishi's biography and interests can be understood, at least in part, as being very much in line with television's emphasis on the writer rather than cinema's interest in stars and director.[32] This emphasis on Kureishi shaped how the film would be understood and used so the conventions of television, in this instance, became a way of publicising the film's appearance in cinemas. This created a somewhat paradoxical situation. As Cook put it, in her review, published as the film hit the cinemas, 'there is no doubt on this evidence that Hanif Kureishi is an exciting new voice in British *television*'.[33]

FROM INDEPENDENT TO MAINSTREAM

As befitting what was now a small, quirky feature film, *My Beautiful Laundrette*, distributed by Romaine Hart's Mainline, opened at two of London's art cinemas, Hart's Screen on the Hill and the newly opened Metro 1, which, appropriately for this controversial film, had been partly financed by the left-wing Greater London Council, then at the height of its rainbow coalition phase.[34] *Screen International* reported that in five days it reached number four in box-office charts with takings of £22,101. It also successfully opened in Edinburgh, taking £4,015 in the first four days. By early December 1985, it had opened at two more London screens, including the more commercially oriented Film Centa 2, where it achieved in takings 'the highest figure the manager has seen in the last nine years'.[35] Thus, although far fewer people saw the film in its opening weeks than would have seen a Film on Four television presentation, the theatrical opening had certainly created that buzz of excitement associated with the cinema.

Reviews were generally favourable, though the rather unlikely trio of the conservative *Sunday Telegraph*, the youthful *New Musical Express* and the radical feminist *Spare Rib* were in different ways unimpressed. A number of those who had reviewed the film at Edinburgh provided second and equally enthusiastic accounts, though, and in general the film was welcomed as 'the sort of independent, low-budget, truly and comprehensively British cinema we signally lack, funny, honest and entertaining'.[36] It was praised for its original handling of contemporary issues, its fresh insight into the Asian community and its ironic critique of Thatcherite economics. A number of critics thought it was a film that would prove to be historically significant in British cinema and Tom Hutchinson made a suggestive comparison: 'For what the film says about the way we live now I consider it to be as important a landmark as *Room at the Top* was 25 years ago.'[37] Significantly, it received reviews outside the mainstream press in *Just 17*, *Ms London* and *Girl about Town*, thus being publicised to young women for whom Daniel Day-Lewis was beginning to be an attraction.

During the first quarter of 1986, *My Beautiful Laundrette* proved that it had cinematic legs. In early January, it was still number four in *Screen International*'s London Top Ten, and it featured in this list until mid-March.[38] In mid-January 1986, two months after the November opening, it was recorded as playing at ten screens in and around London, setting records at Screen Baker Street, Cannon 2 Charing

2. *Cinema publicity. This image of Omar and Johnny outside the trans-
formed launderette was used for film posters and later the video cover.
The resemblance between the launderette and a cinema is discussed in
Chapter 2.* (*Source*: Flashback, courtesy of FilmFour)

Cross Road, the Ritzy, Brixton and Waterman's Centre, Brentford. It
stayed at cinemas for extensive runs; by the beginning of March, it
had run for over seven weeks at the Notting Hill Coronet, grossing
£34,535, and a week later *Screen International* reported that it was still
on at three screens and had run for fourteen weeks at the Charing
Cross and Chelsea Cannons. The film also opened with success outside

London. In mid-February, it took £2,032 in three days at the Bradford
Film Theatre and, at the end of March, *Screen International* headlined
'*Laundrette* still cleaning up in UK' and reported on two 'new all-time
records five months after it first opened – £4,898 for Leeds Hyde Park
Picture House and £3,860 for Birmingham Midlands Arts Centre'. At
this point, it records, there were still fifteen prints of *My Beautiful
Laundrette* playing around the UK and the distributor was 'delighted
with the way it has taken off and held on as it was faced with difficulties
in getting the film distributed in first run situations'.[39] The film disap-
peared from London screens in late June 1986, but quickly returned
in a double bill with *A Letter to Brezhnev* (Bernard, 1985) which ran in
a number of cinemas until mid-October. Although assessments about
the commercial reach of *My Beautiful Laundrette* need to be qualified
by recognising that it was playing mainly in small independent cinemas
or subsidised venues, it was nevertheless clear that the film had been a
substantial success with audiences.

   My Beautiful Laundrette was a commercial success on British exhibition circuits but as important was international recognition. February
1986 saw a successful run in Dublin, but it was the USA which really
mattered. An important screening at the Toronto Film Festival in
September 1985 'garnered more accolades', *Variety* reported, and the
'tortuous route from British TV to Yank Screens' was achieved when the
film was 'snapped … up' for US distribution by Orion Classics, which
also provided 35mm blow-up prints for the UK.[40] The film opened in
New York in March 1986 at an Upper West Side cinema, in the same
week as the more traditionally British *A Room with a View* (1986), which
got a more prestigious screen at Fifth Avenue and 58th Street. In the
USA, its television origins were greeted with some incredulity; 'that
My Beautiful Laundrette could have been conceived as a film for the
small screen', wrote Vincent Canby in the *New York Times*, 'describes
– better than anything else I can think of – the vast difference between
American and English television', while Leonard Quart emphasised that
it was 'no neat American television movie where the ambiguities of
reality are sacrificed to the social problem of the week'.[41] Two months
later, Kureishi exulted that in Los Angeles the film had opened in four
cinemas in a '14 theatre silver-and-neon toilet-tiled complex' and that it
was also 'doing well in Denver, San Francisco, Chicago and Boston'. He
reported also on critical success, noting particularly that 'Pauline Kael,
doyenne of movie critics . . . covered three pages of *The New Yorker*
with description and analysis'.[42] Indeed, Kael, in a typically detailed

and interesting account, did praise it as 'a startling, fresh movie from England'.[43] Picking up on the film's claims to portray contemporary Britain rather than the 'holiday out of time'[44] offered by *A Room with a View*, other reviewers praised *Laundrette* for its individuality. Canby welcomed it as 'a fascinating, eccentric, very personal movie', while Richard Corliss commented that it was 'fast, bold, harsh and primitive like a prodigious student film with equal parts promise and threat'.[45] By the end of June 1986, *Screen International* was able to hail *My Beautiful Laundrette* as a 'major art house hit' in the USA with a gross of $751,465 to that date. Critical acclaim in New York was confirmed when Kureishi won the Best Screenplay awards from the New York Film Critics Circle and the National Society of Film Critics and an Oscar nomination for best screenplay written directly for the screen.

Information about exhibition, then, shows not only that *My Beautiful Laundrette* crossed over from television to cinema but that in commercial and critical terms the move was a great success. Channel 4 decided that the time had come for its delayed television screening and *Laundrette* was screened in the 1986/7 season on 19 February 1987, reaching an audience of 4,336,000. The most popular film screened was *She's Wearing Pink Pyjamas* with Julie Walters, but the season also included the more artistically prestigious *The Company of Wolves* (Jordan, 1984) and the feisty *A Letter to Brezhnev*. The second screening took place on 10 April 1998, achieving, as was usual with second screenings, lower audience figures of 3,550,000.[46]

By this time, though, *My Beautiful Laundrette*'s exhibition history had become something of a byword. It was deemed to be an example of another successfully accomplished cross-over, this time from independent to commercial film. In mainstream terms, *My Beautiful Laundrette*'s reach to popular audiences was highly limited; in terms of British independent cinema, though, it had not only achieved commercial success but had attained a young, diverse and culturally important audience, well beyond the normal reach of avant-garde or independent practices. We can see *Laundrette*'s reputation working in this way at an important conference on black film-making in Britain held at London's Institute of Contemporary Arts in February 1988 under the title 'Black Film British Cinema'. This was just over two years after the film's cinema release and occurred in between its first and second screenings on Channel 4. The conference, organised by cultural critic Kobena Mercer, brought together a wide range of film-makers, cultural theorists, film and video activists and those working in key institutions such as the British Film

Institute and Channel 4. It is at this conference that we can begin to
see how *My Beautiful Laundrette* had, during its successful run, been
accruing layers of significance in debates about black and/or independent film-making in the late eighties. The conference focused on three
rather different films from 1987 – *The Passion of Remembrance*, *Playing
Away* and *Handsworth Songs* – but *My Beautiful Laundrette* keeps pop-
ping up as an exemplary film for left-wing cultural activists.

In this context, *Laundrette*'s television origins tended to be disre-
garded in discussion of its success in cinemas. At the conference, June
Givanni, then a consultant on black and Third World cinema and video,
put it alongside Spike Lee's *She's Gotta Have It* (1986) and spoke of
them both as films that 'have been cited as evidence of wider possibilities
for a mass audience dealing with black themes, issues and perspectives.
In marketing jargon, these relatively low budget feature films have
"crossed over" from small art house audiences to achieve commercial
success in high street cinemas.' Givanni put the success of these films
down to 'the novelty-value of the plots and characterisation' and so
warned that 'such possibilities for black films cannot be predicted and
the potential for "crossover" is limited'.[47] Mercer, in his introduction to
the published conference documents, rather more optimistically ascribed
Laundrette's success to changes in the audience. He proposed the film
as an example of 'a "crossover" phenomenon – whereby material with
apparently marginal subject matter becomes a commercial success in
the marketplace'. This is based, he argued, on 'shifts on the part of
the contemporary audience' since the film does not make claims to a
universal appeal and its success is thus an indication that the market
is breaking up, is no longer 'defined by a monolithic "mass" audience
but by a diversity of audiences whose choices and tastes occasionally
converge'.[48] Thus, a cross-over film can be commercially successful
if it puts together a range of audiences, drawn perhaps by different
elements in the film.

Both Givanni explicitly and Mercer implicitly are talking about
cinema audiences and in neither account is there much acknowledge-
ment of *My Beautiful Laundrette*'s genesis as a television film. Instead,
it is given the same status as *She's Gotta Have It*, the product of a
film school graduate on a shoestring budget. The cross-over this time
is thus perceived to be from art house to a version of mainstream,
and shows how the film had by this stage become exemplary in the
context of independent film-making. It took Colin McCabe, then BFI
Head of Production, to remind the conference that the films they

were discussing were being made for television. He puts *My Beautiful Laundrette*'s success down to the fact that its makers remembered this and that they envisaged their audiences in terms of the television slot doing the commissioning rather than invoking theoretical debates about audience positions.[49]

Channel 4's other slot for experimental film-makers was the Eleventh Hour, and perhaps film academic Jill Forbes had this slot in mind when she suggested that 'Channel 4 is a playground for the children of Marx and Freud'.[50] She might have added Brecht as well, because independent film-makers involved with Channel 4, including a number of the black film-makers at the ICA conference, had been heavily influenced by theoretical debates of the 1970s in which McCabe, in an earlier guise, had been one of those who had identified bourgeois realism as an aesthetic that needed to be undermined, distanced, foregrounded and its narratives generally disrupted. In many ways, this theoretical set of interests had given black work by groups such as Sankofa and the Black Audio Film Collective international success, particularly in North America, but arguably as avant-garde work rather than political interventions.

What *My Beautiful Laundrette* did, however, in crossing over into popularity, was to suggest that disruptive distancing techniques were not prerequisites for a politically progressive film and that dropping such theoreticism would help to attract audiences. Judith Williamson at the ICA insisted polemically on the importance of this breakthrough. She suggested that *My Beautiful Laundrette* was made in an entirely mainstream way and was 'not a formally exciting work'; it was sneered at 'by people who are anti-mainstream' but its importance was that it reached beyond the circles associated with the theoretical film journal *Screen* to people who 'are not at all theoretical' but who 'just love *My Beautiful Laundrette*'.[51] Williamson thus argued that oppositional film-making had to pay attention to questions of pleasure and suggested that the theoretical baggage that was to some extent the orthodoxy in independent film in the 1980s needed to be dropped. Once again, the fact that an explanation for *Laundrette*'s lack of engagement with *Screen* theory might lie in its origins on television is overlooked, although it is likely that Frears and Kureishi were able to make this break precisely because of their different relationship with the independent sector. Nevertheless, if its status as an independent film that crossed over into popularity was somewhat misconceived, such discussion contributed to the view of *My Beautiful Laundrette* as a film that could help to change

ideas about what counted as innovative, political film-making in the
British independent sector.

REALISM AND FANTASY

The account so far may have given the impression that *My Beautiful
Laundrette*'s rise to fortune was smooth and unproblematic. This was not
the case. When Mercer referred to diverse audiences he was thinking of
the reactions to the film from British Asian groups, among film-makers
and in the cultural establishment. Much of this reaction hinged on the
film's relationship with the society it portrayed – its claims, in other
words, to realism or its use of fantasy and surrealism. For *The Spectator* critic, the narrative was rather muddled, 'sometimes conveyed as
social realism and sometimes as fantasy'.[52] But it was not simply that the
film used both approaches. 'Social realism' and 'fantasy' are themselves
loaded terms, and this was another cross-over area, in which the film
was redefined and used in clashes over culture and representation.

Screen International's report on the shoot had trailed the producer
Tim Bevan's comments that *My Beautiful Laundrette* 'somehow reflected
the state of the nation' along with the claims of one of the actors that
it was 'a very, very contemporary film ... It's real.'[53] These terms were
important in setting the context for the film's critical reception. Root's
Edinburgh programme note stressed that it is 'a tale of the eighties';
while not denying other aspects, she pointed to 'the carefully observed
London' in which it is set and the 'tough-minded observation of sleazy
deals and survival-of-the-fittest scams'.[54] Other critics picked up this
realist emphasis on the details of contemporary Britain. The *Observer*
praised it as 'acutely observed' while the *Glasgow Herald* suggested
that Kureishi promised 'to be a unique observer of the way we live'.[55]
Summing up the festival generally, Iain Johnstone commented that
'Reality was most significantly mirrored on screen in *My Beautiful
Laundrette*.'[56]

This realist discourse was maintained by those who were critical
of the film. In Edinburgh, Ian Bell in *The Scotsman* led the opposition. He felt that the film was 'fraudulent'; it 'takes our present hard
times and drapes them over itself like some kind of perversely chic
wallpaper'. He maintained that the film was in fact 'a fantasy', using
the term pejoratively as the opposite of the realistic account other
critics had seen.[57] This theme was repeated by *The Times Educational
Supplement*, whose critic felt that, while the film may have intended 'a

stripping away of the veneer from the "enterprise culture"', what came over was more of a 'baroque fantasy than searing social indictment'.[58] *Girl about Town* commented that the film might be 'too graphic for its own good', while, in a stinging review, *Spare Rib* argued that the film had made 'a laughing stock' of the Asian community at a time when racism was rampant.[59]

This final comment had a sharp, political edge since some British Asians, working within this realist paradigm, reacted strongly to what they took to be an inaccurate and unbalanced depiction of their community. Keith Vaz, a Labour politician in Leicester, criticised the film's focus on a wealthy Pakistani family and complained in a television review programme that 'there were no poor Asians in the film, Asians living on the margins of poverty, which is what we have in this country ... There is mass overcrowding in the inner city areas where the Asian community is.'[60] This was a complaint about the film's representativeness based on an assumption that it would be understood as speaking for a united community and that its characters would be taken for typical members of that community. For British Asian film-makers working in a documentary or social-realist tradition, the film posed specific problems. Mahmood Jamal, a member of the first Asian film and video collective set up in 1984 and producer of *Majdhar*, which was shown in Channel 4's Eleventh Hour slot in 1985, complained that *My Beautiful Laundrette* expressed 'all the prejudices that this society has felt about Asians and Jews – that they are money grabbing, scheming, sex-crazed people'; he criticised Kureishi as an example of an Asian intellectual 'laundered by the British university system' who 'reinforce stereotypes of their own people for a few, cheap laughs'.[61] This hostility extended to overseas screenings when the film was picketed in New York by the Pakistani Action Committee, and did not subside readily. In 1988, Perminder Dhillon-Kashyap criticised *My Beautiful Laundrette* for 'subtly rework[ing] stereotypes, thereby adding an "authenticity" to them', and picked up a common complaint about the representation of Asian women, commenting particularly on the way Rita Wolf as Omar's cousin Tania bares 'her breasts to the voyeuristic gaze'.[62] Sarita Malik later summarised this debate, suggesting that 'the most publicised responses to the film refused to see it as anything but realist or the characters as determined by anything other than their ethnic identity'.[63]

But attacks on the film's realism did nothing to damage its growing status as an innovative, political film. For the intellectual and cultural groupings represented at the ICA, claims that films could or should represent reality were highly dubious and strong elements of anti-realism and fantasy were therefore to be welcomed. Kureishi himself had taken a combative approach when publicising the film, suggesting that the call from those such as Vaz, far from being a plea for realism, was a demand for the kind of positive images that required the writer to act 'as public relations officer, as hired liar'.[64] Kureishi expressed this in terms of trying to 'make the characters rounded and human', terms that might have been incorporated into an extension of what realism might mean in this context, but his refusal to be 'a spokesman for the Asian community'[65] meant that, at the ICA, despite Williamson's emphasis on the film's mainstream qualities, *My Beautiful Laundrette* could be folded back into the anti-realist, theoretical framework associated with *Screen*, though perhaps in a more generous way than had been characteristic in the late 1970s. Thus, Julian Henriques, in an article reprinted for the ICA documentation, used the film as an example of 'non-realist work' to 'provoke discussion on some of the realist assumptions we take for granted in black art'.[66] He conceded that there were some difficulties over stereotyping but nevertheless considered that *My Beautiful Laundrette* was successful precisely because it was 'a fantasy expressing the feelings, contradictions and imagination of the characters, rather than any attempt to reflect reality' (p. 19). Picking up Kureishi's emphasis on the artist's role, Henriques argued that realism produces 'endless discussion of the need for positive images to counter the negative stereotypes', which 'denies the role of art altogether' (p. 20). Instead, Henriques placed the emphasis on breaks and contradictions, language familiar to many at the ICA through film theory's reworking of Brecht, and suggested that 'the success of the film was its break with the realist tradition' which had allowed it to take 'the central imaginative leap' of focusing on the 'multiple contradiction of a love affair between two men, two races and two politics'. Only by dealing with 'the issue of contradiction' in this way could the film, through its presentation of an 'imaginative, contradictory world', point to the 'possibility of change' (p. 19).

In his introduction to the published papers, Mercer re-emphasised the importance of freeing black film-makers from the '"burden of represen-tation"', pointing to 'a widening range of strategic interventions against the master codes of the race relations narrative'.[67] Black artists do not speak *for* but *from* ethnic communities, and debates over films such as *My Beautiful Laundrette* draw attention to 'image-making' as 'an important

arena of cultural contestation'; it is the very oppositional quality of
black film-making, its refusal to provide unified or unifying images,
which exposes the way in which the 'traditional structures of cultural
value and national identity' are becoming 'fractured, fragmented and ...
de-centred' (p. 5). Mercer suggested that the contradictory responses to
My Beautiful Laundrette had wider repercussions and fed into a complex
debate about black independent cinema and the nature of and need for
cultural interventions about national identity.

The film's ambiguous referential status, the way it criss-crossed
between realism and fantasy, its claims to be both a representation of the
state of Thatcher's nation and a fragmented evocation of a contradictory
love affair, made *My Beautiful Laundrette* a contested set of elements
in what was often a difficult and sometimes a very bitter debate. For,
as Mercer himself later ruefully recognised, the ICA conference was
itself controversial in terms of representation:

> Through an entirely contingent set of circumstances none of the Asian
> speakers invited could participate, and yet among some members of
> the audience this absence was interpreted as the outcome of a crypto-
> nationalist exclusion of British Asian voices and viewpoints ... because
> it was the 'first' event of its kind at that particular institutional space,
> there was a general expectation that it would be totally 'representa-
> tive', and would say all there was to be said about black filmmaking
> in Britain.[68]

Despite a reminder of this context, though, it is clear that the conference did provide a forum for the debate about the negative aspects of
realism and representation to move into a more positive discussion of
future possibilities for black identity. To this move, also, *My Beautiful
Laundrette* made a contribution.

IDENTITY AND HYBRIDITY

If its anti-realist contradictions and refusals were elements that allowed
the film to be welcomed in independent film circles, the way in which
it could be used in theoretical debates about identity increased its exemplary status. As Henriques said, the film took cross-overs as its subject
matter – 'a love affair between two men, two races and two politics'[69]
– and thus was available to be incorporated into the theories of identity
and hybridity being developed by, among others, Paul Gilroy and Stuart
Hall.[70] It was through this critical discourse that *My Beautiful Laundrette*

was consolidated as an 'important' film in its controlled crossing of the 'frontiers between gender, race, ethnicity, sexuality and class'.[71]

In his Edinburgh review Derek Malcolm commented that, despite dealing with important 'racial issues and attitudes', the film was the 'absolute opposite of a tract. In fact, it is a comedy with a gay theme.'[72] It is perhaps worth noting that the question of gay representation on Channel 4 had been controversial from the outset. The channel had a mandate to provide programmes for groups not catered for by other broadcasters but the documentaries, magazine shows and dramas aimed at gay and lesbian viewers caused offence to others. Audience researchers in its early years reported that 'no question of morality, however, has come anywhere near in significance in illustrating the potential difficulties in fulfilling the channel's mandate as that of the treatment of gay and lesbian issues'.[73]

So *My Beautiful Laundrette* was operating in controversial waters, but those critics who liked the film felt that the gay relationship was at the joyous heart of the story. Characteristically, Kureishi once again set the tone for this response. Whereas he used the press to point out that in addressing race he had deliberately shown 'the violence, hostility and contempt directed against black people'[74] as a challenge to complacent assumptions of British tolerance, he suggested that the gay relationship arose out of the characters: 'When the boys just kept wanting to do it with each other in the script, I let them. It seemed perfectly natural, not strange or particularly interesting. I hadn't set out to explore issues around gayness ... I preferred just to take it for granted, the way we do in our lives now.'[75]

It is this straightforward expression of desire which was welcomed in the debate about the film's representation of a gay relationship in the liberal press. Philip French commented that the love affair was consummated 'with passion, conviction and tenderness', and Cook observed that the personal relationship between the two young men was marked by 'moments of tenderness, warmth and humour'.[76] *The Listener* praised 'the easy, un-emphatic handling of homosexual love' and, in the USA, Quart commented that 'there isn't a hint of self-consciousness or intimation of anything psychologically problematic about their sexuality'.[77]

This theme of natural and enjoyable sexual expression was taken up in reports more overtly addressed to homosexual and lesbian audiences. *Gay Times* praised the film for making the gay affair 'so perfectly "natural"'.[78] Mark Finch, in the left-wing listings magazine *City Limits*, summed it up as 'one of the most pleasurable gay representations ever to appear in cinema' and recorded 'a genuine frisson when Omar and Johnny kiss for the first time. No thunderous music, no suspenseful high-angle shot, no angst, just a thrilled gasp from the audience.'[79]

Using the film to remind readers of other more punishing or anxious gay and lesbian representations, Finch took up the question of the burden of representation and argued against the 'impossible responsibility' placed on gay film-makers 'to fully represent minority communities'. He commended the refusal of social realism and the 'multiplicity of the gay experience, full of humour and passion' (p. 14). Once again, Kureishi shapes this debate, providing a comment highlighted in the layout of this article: 'if it gives one person an erection and makes one person laugh that's good enough for me', he is quoted as saying; 'I want to cause laughter and sexual excitement at the same time' (p. 14). Thus, in this initial address to gay audiences, the invitation is to pleasure rather than political debate.

From the outset, then, *My Beautiful Laundrette* was understood and applauded in a critical context that valued the film's attitude to gay sexual attraction. At the ICA, however, these critical comments are in turn placed in a theoretical position that puts *My Beautiful Laundrette* at the heart of cultural debates about identity. Stuart Hall's contribution used the discussion about black independent cinema to take forward ideas about subjectivity and hybridity. Reflecting on debates about black representation, Hall did not deny the importance of challenging stereotypes, resisting objectification and drawing attention to the unequal access to production for black film-makers. Hall argued, though, that a shift was taking place in black cultural experience which did not replace the earlier moment, but might reposition or displace it. The problem with work on representation had been that it had been premised on the '"black experience", as a singular and unifying framework', and the need to critique 'the fetishization, objectification and negative figuration'[80] which are a feature of the representation of the black subject. Hall suggested that a new phase of work would see 'the end of the innocent notion of the essential black subject' and instead would develop an approach in which 'black' itself is understood as a constructed and diverse term, 'essentially a politically and culturally *constructed* category ... which therefore has no guarantees in Nature'. *My Beautiful Laundrette*, with other films, made it clear, Hall argued, that 'the question of the black subject cannot be represented without reference to the dimensions of class, gender, sexuality and ethnicity' (p. 28). Drawing on his own sense of being a migrant, he

proposed a new 'politics of representation' that would entail an awareness of the black experience as 'a *diaspora* experience' (p. 29), rooted in
movement and marked not by separation but by processes of mixing, of
'unsettling, recombination, hybridization and "cut-and-mix"' (p. 30). In
this formulation, difference is understood as 'a positional, conditional and
conjunctural' concept (p. 29) which allows for common struggle without
suppressing the 'heterogeneity of interests and identities' involved. This
makes it possible, and indeed essential, for the central issues of race to
be 'constantly crossed and recrossed by the categories of class, of gender
and ethnicity' (p. 28). It is this theoretical shift which gives *My Beautiful
Laundrette*, with its central gay relationship and its in-between characters,
its status as an exemplary text in Hall's account. The essay ends with a
call for 'a politics of criticism' which is able to say 'why *My Beautiful
Laundrette* is one of the most riveting and important films produced by
a black writer in recent years and precisely for the reason that made it
so controversial: its refusal to represent the black experience in Britain
as monolithic, self-contained, sexually stabilized and always "right-on"
– in a word always and only positive' (p. 30).

Other speakers echoed this call, and the publication of the ICA
document and the reprinting of Hall's address in other collections
made these ideas available to a wider public in film education as well
as in the independent film sector. Mercer reinforced Hall's emphasis on
identity as contingent and hybrid, emphasising 'the many-voicedness
and variousness of British cultural identity, *as it is lived*',[81] setting that
against the myths of the colonial past exemplified by *Chariots of Fire*.
This concept of identity, of course, chimes with postmodern emphases
on anti-essentialism and difference; in that sense, what was being proposed was that the formation of black identity was not unique but
exemplary, a complex version of the process by which any identity
is formed and claimed across 'the frontiers of gender, race, ethnicity,
sexuality and class'. What was needed, Hall had said, was 'a recognition
that we all speak from a particular place, out of a particular history,
out of a particular culture, without being contained by that position
as "ethnic artists" or film-makers. We are all, in that sense, ethnically
located and our ethnic identities are crucial to our subjective sense of
who we are.'[82]

Hall's 'we are all' is somewhat ambiguous, addressed to the mixed
audience at the conference but referring specifically and rather uncom-
fortably to '"ethnic artists" or film-makers'. His theoretical elaboration
of diversity, difference and subjectivity, though, was claimed by a wider

audience in cultural studies and beyond for whom work on identity became crucial in the 1990s.

As we have seen, *My Beautiful Laundrette* always existed in a discursive context of debate, discussion and controversy, whether it be about the relationship between cinema and television, about questions of realism and representation or the experience of living as a Pakistani or a gay man in Thatcher's Britain. The ICA conference, I would argue, marked the point at which the film was clearly defined within the discourse surrounding it. 'The possibilities of interpretation', to use Barbara Klinger's phrase, have become 'streamlined'[83] and the film becomes a text in a critical and controversial debate on the cultural left about questions of representation and identity. A way of understanding the film, of 'reading' it through this kind of debate, has become established, and we shall see how that developed in Chapter 3. But inevitably, perhaps, as the film became exemplary in a political and theoretical debate, its complexity and pleasures were assumed rather than themselves the subject of detailed analysis. At this point, therefore, I want to turn to a close examination of the film's formal qualities and aesthetic pleasures.

TWO
Transformations:
Film Analysis

This analysis of the film does not lose sight of the cross-over themes underpinning the previous section which are woven into and, I hope, illuminated by the more detailed textual approach which follows. The first part of this section looks at the way in which the film is organised, identifying key narrative strands and examining how *My Beautiful Laundrette*'s rather loose stories eventually move towards a more conventional climax; the film's racial and sexual themes emerge through this analysis, though I suggest that they are treated rather differently in terms of narrative organisation. The second part looks at how the film organises its narrative spaces, an approach that allows for a discussion of the film's aesthetics in the context of its utopian discourse. Finally, I shall look at acting and star image, highlighting key moments of performance and examining the effect of the film on the careers of the main actors. Overall, this detailed account, which returns to particular scenes at various points in order to weave in new elements, involves reflection as well as analysis. This seems appropriate since, although at first much in the film seems to rely on chance and coincidence, the process of reflection shows how much the film's pleasures lie in the way in which events, images, sound and characters are imbricated and layered.

arranged in an overlapping way

NARRATIVE ANALYSIS

Before embarking on a detailed account of the film's narrative, it is worth making some general points about what kind of narrative *My Beautiful Laundrette* is. In saying that it has a loose structure, I am suggesting that, using Tzvetvan Todorov's broad distinction, *My Beautiful Laundrette* is a 'narrative of contiguity' in which events provoke unforeseen consequences which in turn take us forward again to an unknown destination; Todorov contrasts this with the 'narrative of substitutions' in which an originating event (often a death or a crime) is explored and alternative solutions tested out until the explanation that matches the initial event is found and can be told.[1] The narrative of substitutions is organised around a past event, which often becomes the focus of the hero's obsession and which provides the central organising point for the story; the narrative of contiguity is more open to sidetracking as events occur and the hero tends to move through a series of adventures before resolution is reached. The resolution of this kind of narrative is less likely to tie up all the loose ends since the point of the story is to move forward rather than look back. In terms of cinema, film noir and the detective story are narratives of substitutions while the Western and the romance are often narratives of contiguity.

I do not intend here to give a full account of the plot but rather to point to how the story can be understood, and open up the rhythms, repetitions and cross-overs that contribute to its meaning. Four strands intertwine in the narrative organisation of *My Beautiful Laundrette*. Two of these are major strands, crucial to the overall narrative effect. The first is the story of the gay romance, the establishment of a relationship between Omar and Johnny, a story that focuses on the two main protagonists and the possibilities of their coming together. The second main strand tells the story of Omar's business activity with his uncle Nasser and, in doing so, places each protagonist in his social context – in Omar's case, that of his family, in Johnny's case, the more restricted milieu of the gang. Two secondary narrative lines can also be identified. In the first of these, Rachel, Nasser's mistress, and Tania, Nasser's daughter, are set up as outliers whose concerns cannot be fitted into the main storylines and who therefore have to leave; although they are in different positions in relation to the family and the business, they are linked by this structural relationship to the main stories. Finally, and most tentatively, there is the story of the brothers, Nasser and Papa, a story partly lost in the past and one in which a different conclusion is hinted at but aborted.

The narrative starts before the credits by plunging us into an event without explanation or introduction to the characters. In a derelict house, a character who will be named as Salim organises the eviction of Johnny, who will be one of the heroes of the film, and his friend, Genghis. Johnny decides that it is 'Too early in the morning'[2] to fight and the pair escape out of the window, pausing only at the washing line for Johnny to pick up some clothes. It will take some time for the film to refer back to this scene and establish quite how it fits in.

Nevertheless, looking back we can see how this prologue affects a number of narrative points. Salim is clearly marked as the disruptive agent in the film; he is responsible for the eviction and for the violence that accompanies it. The business theme is thus introduced and, in its worst aspects, connected to Salim. The scene also introduces Johnny as a figure who can control things, even though we will have to wait some time before he reappears as a key figure in the gay romance thread. Most significantly, though, although the two do not recognise each other later, the scene establishes Salim and Johnny as antagonists, a fact that will increase in importance in the final minutes as the film moves to its conclusion. This seemingly artless opening, an everyday incident in the life of property owner and squatter, thus serves to point the way to narrative resolution.

The unelaborate credits then unfold, simple letters against a background of pastel-coloured washing machines. The title is framed by two black lines indicating the curves of a washing machine port hole, the letters spin into a blur and the music is a comic rendering of water glugging down a plug hole.[3]

The next scene introduces Omar and Papa, establishing Omar in his role as carer for his father, a less dynamic role and one more integrated into his family than that of Johnny. A framed photo economically suggests that the woman of the family is gone (we learn later of her possible suicide), and the drained bottle indicates Papa's drink problem. Nevertheless, it is the passive and enervated Papa who initiates two main narrative threads. A phone call to his brother Nasser sets Omar up with a job and also raises the question of romance; 'try to fix him up with a nice girl', Papa tells Nasser, 'I'm not sure if his penis is in full working order.'

The narrative now works to move Omar into this new world of the family business. Omar arrives at the garage and is at first taken by Salim for an interloper. Properly welcomed by Nasser, however, he is given an initial test of manual work, washing cars. Immediately afterwards, in a scene in a bar, Nasser introduces him to his business philosophy – the 'one essential thing ... You just have to know how to squeeze the tits of the system' – and reassures him of his place in the family – 'You're like a son to me.' Omar settles vigorously into cleaning windscreens but is hailed by Nasser for another task – 'help me with accounts'. At the end of this sequence, Nasser sets up the next move for Omar, announcing 'I've got a big challenge lined up for him' and telling him to come to his house to hear about it.

3. *Rachel as an intermediary between Omar and his uncle, Nasser.* (*Source:* courtesy of FilmFour)

At the same time as Omar is being tested in the business, he is also being introduced to Rachel. In these short scenes, Rachel is established both as a sexual being (we see what Omar only overhears, Rachel's enthusiastic sex with Nasser) and a motherly woman. At this point in the narrative, she is at ease, casually confident with Salim and acting as an intermediary between Nasser and Omar. In the scene at the bar, for instance, Rachel sits between the two men and explains Nasser's convoluted metaphors to Omar; 'he's saying he wants to help you', she says, smiling. Similarly, Rachel eases Omar's way into business by prompting Nasser to give him a car. At this stage, then, Rachel is so far inside the business family that Nasser includes her in his reassurance to Omar: 'You're like a son to me', he says, adding, with a look to Rachel, 'to both of us'. Omar responds to Rachel's intimate tones with enthusiastic and safe flirting. The narrative strand dealing with Rachel has thus been introduced but she seems to be part of the stable situation rather than the disruptive problem often represented in film narratives by the sexually active woman.

The short scene that follows serves as a bridge to the next stage of Omar's incorporation into the business and defines Papa's main role as commentator on his son's actions. As Omar gets ready for his trip to Nasser's house, Papa sardonically enquires what it is about cleaning cars which makes him so ecstatic, and reminds him that his main goal should be to go to college. Omar is non-committal, but a brief glimpse of the new car as he arrives at Nasser's house reminds us of what he really wants, although he hasn't fully expressed it yet. When he arrives at the house we are introduced, along with Omar, to various members of the family, including Tania, Nasser's daughter, Bilquis, his wife, and Cherry, Salim's wife, who taunts Omar for knowing nothing about Pakistan and being an 'in-between'. Omar gets the news about working in the launderette and, with this specific plot reference planted, the scene also reinforces the business/family nexus by showing Omar as Nasser's possible heir.

At the same time, other narratives are referred to in similarly tangential ways. The story of the two brothers is taken back into the past as Omar overhears the end of the story about his father which Nasser is telling his male audience; the punch line is not that Papa was locked out in the freezing cold with a naked woman but that he was foolish enough to marry her. The question of Omar's marriage to Tania (which will of course prove a red herring) is raised again when she makes it clear to him how bored and frustrated she is with family life. Tania's connections with Rachel begin to be established at the same time when, at the end of the sequence in the house, she questions Omar about Nasser's mistress.

Omar's willingness to be involved with the family means that he agrees when Cherry asks Omar to drive them both home, the first of two fateful drives Omar takes with Salim. As they wait under a bridge, the car is surrounded by members of the gang, the South London counterpoint to the Pakistani family. This scene of danger and threat is the setting for the initiation of the gay romance strand. Omar, much less frightened than Cherry and Salim, sees Johnny standing aloof from the attack. In this parody of eyes meeting 'across a crowded room', Omar is drawn out of the car and away from his new family to re-establish contact with his old friend. Johnny in fact offers him immediate action as a couple, away from both gangs, but Omar now remembers his commitments elsewhere and, laughing, goes back to the car. Thus, Johnny is established as another attraction for Omar, but one potentially in opposition to his business ambitions.

Omar returns to Papa who again provides a jaundiced comment on his enthusiasms, dismissing Johnny and contemptuously asking Omar to 'illustrate your washing methods' on a piece of dirty laundry. For the first time Omar expresses anger with his father, a sign that he is moving away from him.

But the next three scenes show that the ease with which Omar has entered the family business is deceptive. The run-down nature of the launderette is established when Nasser shows Omar round, and Nasser's amused agreement that Omar can be the manager indicates that there might be difficulties ahead. This is immediately confirmed in the next scene when Salim comes to the launderette. Omar asks for help – 'I'm afraid I've made a fool of myself' – and Salim responds that Nasser has given him 'a dead duck'. Salim's offer of help, however, commits Omar to a dubious errand to collect videos from the airport.

My Beautiful Laundrette, despite some of the trappings of gangsters and drugs, is not a thriller and so it does not attempt to generate tension over Omar's first job for Salim. Instead, the narrative significance of the event is to confirm Salim's evil nature and to indicate the possibility of Omar using this to his advantage. Omar makes the collection offscreen but the interaction with Salim is the subject of an extended scene. At first, Salim with his joint, gold chain and shower hat, is treated as a figure of fun and the scene suggests that Omar's successful mission has made him 'one of us'. But when Omar, in his role as innocent fool, tries out the video and starts asking questions, Salim turns into a pantomime villain, pushing Omar to the ground and, in a dramatic close-up, literally grinding his face into the carpet.

These scenes take Omar farther into the family business, but throughout them there are also reminders of the romance story, which is still latent. After Omar has taken possession of the launderette, a rather confusing high shot of a cityscape (omitted in the DVD) shows gang members apparently distributing leaflets while Johnny stands aloof in the middle of the road. Delivering the videos, Omar passes the time while Salim gets dressed by leaving a phone message for Johnny. After the scene with Salim, Omar comes across two members of the gang and asks after Johnny. They immediately warn him off – 'Piss off back to the jungle, wog boy' – but Omar remains impervious. Contact between the two is re-established in the next scene as Papa complains furiously about Omar's inexpert toenail cutting. Papa tries to phone Nasser to extricate Omar from the business world; instead, Johnny puts a call through and a delighted Omar rushes off to meet him.

Johnny now enters the launderette and almost immediately challenges Salim's power. As the scene opens, Johnny looks round as Omar explains his ambitions and says he wants Johnny to work with him. In contrast to the previous scene, Omar's attitude is rather cold and contemptuous, treating Johnny as a worker who takes orders – 'Start by clearing those bastards out.' Johnny throws the kids out, just as Salim arrives, an action that refers back to and reverses the opening scene. Salim takes Omar to the back to offer him another 'little errand' but Omar makes it clear that he and Johnny are now working together.

This time we see the 'errand', though the very brief scene in the hotel room is somewhat confusing initially and the joking way in which the carrier pulls off his beard plays the scene for comedy. This is reinforced when Omar returns exuberantly to the launderette to show Johnny the beard and to suggest double-crossing Salim. Omar is eager to raise money to transform the launderette, while Johnny is more thoughtful about how the plan that he should sell the drugs affects his previous decision not to go on being 'a bad boy'. The romance plot is here on hold as Omar drives the business plot on. The next two scenes complete this narrative event. Omar, wearing the beard, interrupts Salim's act as the socially smooth host of a dinner party; Salim is puzzled and, having heard Omar deny that anything odd happened on the way there, threatens that something may yet happen on the way back. Typically this is not followed up, though Salim's implicit power is shown in a high-angle shot from his balcony as he watches Omar's white car drive off. The next scene continues the pattern of playing down the drug dealing and, like the hotel transaction, is an example of how the film uses a brief, wordless scene to stand for a quite complex and potentially dangerous transaction. The drugs sale is filmed in medium shot, with no dialogue, and 'covered' by the lights and sounds of a disco. As a reminder of the romance plot, another red herring is set up as a tease. At the beginning of the scene, Omar comments on a 'nice girl' who is dancing on her own; the end of the scene shows Omar leaning against a pillar smoking while Johnny slow-dances with the same girl.

The family business plot, which will enable the launderette to be transformed, is now set up. The narrative then turns to Johnny, both to bring him into this plot and to move the romance plot forward. Once again Nasser's house is the site for the criss-crossing of plots. Salim and Tania both treat Omar as a businessman, Salim warning him 'Don't fuck your uncle's launderette' while Tania, though she defends Omar against Salim, privately tells him that 'you're greedy like my father'. Omar reports to Nasser that the launderette will go well because 'I've hired a bloke of outstanding strength'. Nasser is delighted by this reversal of the usual Pakistani/white relationships and Omar continues to treat Johnny as a worker, leaving him waiting in the drive – 'he's lower class, he won't come in without being asked unless it's a burglary' – until he is ready to introduce him. Nasser asks Johnny to help him move out some 'bastard tenants', what he calls 'unscrewing ... your favourite subject, Salim'. Salim is angry that Nasser is giving away business secrets and, as Nasser's crony Zaki comments, is bringing Johnny into 'some family business'. The scene ends with Nasser calling for champagne to toast their business success, 'to Thatcher and your beautiful launderette'.

But if the focus is on the business plot, with Johnny rather resentfully brought into it, the other plots are also woven in. The scene starts with a reminder of Omar's other loyalties as he begs Nasser to tell him stories of Papa's past. Tania, though at her most content here, continues to distance herself from her father and the business and to appeal to Omar as a source of escape. Most crucially, though, Omar begins to deviate from his single-minded pursuit of business success. When he responds to Salim's warning with 'much good can come of fucking', it is clear that he is not just talking about business. And when Omar and Tania bring Johnny into the house, Omar's gesture of brushing his hand against Johnny's face – 'Eyelash'– is the first deliberate touch between them and alerts Tania and the audience to other possibilities.

These possibilities are now taken up as Omar and Johnny walk back to the launderette, excited about creating 'a launderette as big as the Ritz'. Johnny pulls Omar to him and the pair kiss in a passionate embrace which, as the couple and the camera move, is caught in the light, the dark and the light again. Immediately, though, noise alerts them to danger, and Johnny runs to find members of the gang outside the launderette. He stops them doing any damage but the violent language and the sound of a knife scraping the pavement make the danger clear. 'There's no one else who really wants you,' warns Genghis, but there is, of course, and the romance plot continues as the music provides the link between this scene and the next, which opens with a long shot of Omar and Johnny kissing in the open-top car – an idyllic scene, but again the romance is thwarted, this time by Omar's memories of how Johnny and his friends behaved towards his father. Johnny leaves the car to pad through the derelict streets and haul himself up into another squat. Omar goes home to his father, dead asleep with the vodka bottle beside him. Omar caresses his face but expresses his frustration by hurling the bottle across the railway tracks.

The business plot and the romance now being fully set up, the film begins to emphasise Salim and Johnny as competing forces in a series of scenes, that also build up to the opening of the launderette. Salim

4. *Rachel and Nasser waltz in the transformed launderette.* (*Source*: Flash-back, courtesy of FilmFour)

is shown outside the launderette, watching Johnny decorating and Omar paying him with a hug as well as a note tucked into his pocket. Puzzled, Salim asks Nasser about the launderette's finances, a discussion interrupted by the arrival of Johnny, who presses his face against the window in a reminder of the gang members menacing Salim's car. Salim taunts an impassive Johnny so that Nasser has to intervene to take him off to work, 'unscrewing' an undesirable tenant. Nasser offers Johnny a room in return for keeping an eye on the house, pulling him farther into the family nexus. Back at the launderette, Johnny completes the final decoration of the exterior with its light bulbs and neon signs while he and Omar disagree about Salim – 'I wish Salim could see this.' 'Why? He's after us.' Chords of music take us from this scene to the next, the grand opening.

The opening of the launderette is the most complex scene in the film. Up until this point, the different stories seem rather unconnected, and the scenes open and close quite abruptly. The opening of the launderette acts as a climax to the romance and business plots but also indicates how they are going to unravel. Compared with the earlier part of the film, with its short, free-standing scenes, the opening smoothly picks up threads from all four plots and incorporates bit characters and minor events into a complex scenario. We can trace out how the four plot lines are imbricated here. The scene provides the clearest expression of the gay romance theme as Omar and Johnny make love as the crowds gather outside the newly decorated launderette. Underlining this coming together is the romantic dance of Nasser and Rachel, who waltz round the launderette in a bitter-sweet moment which marks the high spot of their relationship. The interweaving of disparate elements is marked by the fact that it is the outsider Rachel who cuts the ribbon and opens the new venture. Nasser's presence, and later that of the brooding Salim, justifies Omar's pride in his business achievement ('We thought we'd do the area a favour,' boasts Nasser, taking the credit for the launderette) and, for a moment, the success of the business seems assured as Omar discusses taking on two more launderettes from Zaki.

But other stories break across this resolution. Papa's absence has, from the beginning, troubled Omar, and now Tania and Rachel as the two outliers begin to pull apart the accommodation between business, family and romance which Omar and Johnny have tentatively achieved. Tania and Rachel have been linked by Tania's questions to Omar and she now expresses her hostility directly by declaring, 'I don't like women who live off men.' Rachel gently points out the similarity of their positions – 'Tell me, who do you live off?' – while Nasser orders Omar to sort things out – 'Marry her ... Your penis works, doesn't it?' Out in the street, as dusk falls, Rachel blames Nasser for Tania's presence and walks out of the scene. Later, standing at the door as if poised to leave again, Omar follows Nasser's orders and asks Tania to marry him. In the background, Salim watches while the gang members taunt Johnny about football and loyalty.

With characteristic narrative economy, the break-up of the lovers by their respective claimants is achieved quickly. Salim, as swift as Iago, tells Johnny of Omar's marriage offer and takes Omar out into the street to discuss the money that he 'stole'. As Salim threatens to take the launderette away, Johnny rejoins the gang and goes off with them. This brief scene thus reopens narrative lines regarding both business and romance which seemed to have been closed off and, with the deadline of the launderette opening now in the past, another narrative deadline is set up – Salim wants his money back by the time of Nasser's annual party.

In some senses, the film now starts again, returning to the ground that has already been worked over but exploring it more fully. Omar goes looking for Johnny again, finding him alone in his room as a noisy party rages around the house. Johnny challenges Omar's business interests but

Omar returns their relationship to that of employer/employee – 'Now you're washing my floor and that's the way I like it.' Omar pulls back from his romantic connections with Johnny, claiming 'I don't want to see you for a little while', and Johnny goes back to the launderette alone, where he abruptly turns off the sad strains of *Madame Butterfly*, which one of the customers has been 'conducting'.

As he does so, there is an unexpected visitor. Papa belatedly arrives for the opening and is alternately arrogant and pleading with Johnny. This is the only point when we see Papa outside the flat, and he gives the launderette some kind of commendation – 'not a bad dump'. Although he is uncompromising in his disappointment with Johnny, he pleads for his help in persuading Omar to go back to college. Papa, who had initiated Omar's entry into the world of business and family, is now helpless to pull him out of it. There is no evidence that Johnny picks up this plea, confirming again Papa's irrelevance to the business plot.

Instead, Johnny turns up at Nasser's house again in response to Omar's call. Two narrative lines are now driven forward. While Nasser's wife, Bilquis, tries to put a spell on Rachel, Omar and Johnny agree to commit a burglary so as to get money to repay Salim and, in doing so, declare a more personal commitment to each other. As with the drug dealing, the burglary is so briefly sketched that its purpose as a plot device is clear; getting the money for the deadline is achieved and Omar and Johnny have been brought back together.

Once again, though, they separate, this time at Nasser's party. Unlike the launderette opening, the party serves to reinforce differences and, in the opening moments, Johnny reminds Omar that the question of marriage to Tania still lies between them. The split is reinforced as Omar spends his time in business conversations while Johnny fools about with Tania. Omar, growing in confidence, refuses to turn down any option, however implausible. In the debacle generated by Johnny and Tania at the end, Omar tries to placate his uncle by declaring that he and Tania will marry 'any day now', an offer Tania vehemently turns down. Despite the clear hostility between them, Omar leaves the party with both Johnny and Salim, seizing Johnny's hand but announcing that he needs Salim 'for something I have in mind'.

For the second car journey Salim is driving. Omar wins Salim's approval for his business expansion – 'You're a smart bastard' – though Johnny's figure, in the back seat but positioned between them visually, indicates his opposition. The car stops again under the bridge and, in a reverse of the previous episode, Salim aggressively attacks the gang, hitting Moose. The scene ends with Genghis looking after the car and apparently recognising those in it. The clash between Salim and the gang is now direct and no longer needs Johnny and Omar as intermediaries.

The dénouement begins slowly to pull in the threads as the gang prepares for revenge. Though Johnny is no longer with his old friends, he explicitly refuses to enter into business that involves 'that scum Salim', and he can be seen slouching in the car in the background as Omar inspects Zaki's launderette and agrees to take it over. Johnny sees Moose on crutches in the wing mirror and drives off. Back at the launderette, Genghis is patrolling the flat roof with a club of wood in his hands, while down in the street other gang members wait. The remaining scenes, up until the fight actually begins, are punctuated by such menacing shots. Before this confrontation, though, Tania and Rachel have to be expelled. Tania arrives in the launderette to tell Johnny she is going and to ask him to join her, warning him that the family will 'eat you'. Johnny makes it clear he is staying because of Omar, making explicit what has not been said so far – 'I couldn't leave him. Not now. Don't ask me to. Ever touched him?' In the meantime, Rachel, in an empty bar, is breaking off with Nasser, pointing to her rash and remarking sadly, 'It's not possible to enjoy being hated so much. Your wife is a brilliant woman.' Rachel walks away into the background, leaving Nasser alone.

The film is now building much more coherently from action to action, with the connections between them made clear. On Rachel's departure, Nasser goes to visit Papa and in a series of brief scenes, intercut with the violence at the launderette, the story of the brothers, indicated in fleeting references earlier, is now explored. On entering the flat, Nasser finds his brother lying still and for a moment thinks he is dead. Nasser touches his hand and Papa rises into his tearful embrace. Papa suggests that they should go home but Nasser, still resilient, sees possibilities – 'compared with everywhere it's a little heaven here'. But Papa, for the first time in the film, tries to explore someone else's feelings and asks why he's so unhappy. Nasser moves to the window – 'Rachel has left me and I don't know what to do' – and then out to the balcony, where Papa joins him, stroking him gently on the arm. Nasser confesses he is 'finished', meaning his business as well as Rachel, but further confidences are prevented by the sight of Tania on the platform and her magical disappearance under cover of a passing train. Nasser shouts, Papa retreats inside the flat and Nasser can only look at him, abandoned.

The tales of Rachel, Tania and the brothers are thus completed in tender counterpoint to the violence at the launderette. In Omar's absence on business with Zaki, Johnny is joined by Salim, who waits for his return. Outside the window, the gang attacks Salim's car, the car that ran them down, and when Salim intervenes they turn on him, Genghis jumping down from the roof where he has been prowling. Johnny waits but finally, as Salim's head is smashed against the car, he comes out of the launderette and pulls Genghis off. The two former friends fight, despite Johnny's protests that he doesn't want to, and Omar and Zaki, coming round the corner, see Johnny being battered. Sirens sound and the gang retreats as Salim crawls away. Omar tries to protect Johnny and hold his bloody face as a gang member returns with a dustbin which he holds over the heads of the couple and then turns to crash it though the glass window of the launderette.

The main characters of the business plot have been defeated, Nasser by the two women whom he tried to keep apart, Salim by the 'scum' he despised. The film makes no attempt to tie up the question of whether Omar can succeed in the business enterprise he has so keenly pursued. Instead, the final scenes of the film return to the gay romance and offer a resolution based on the couple, caught in a moment of pleasure. Initially, it appears that Johnny will go since he refuses Omar's teasing words and the touch that had previously kept him there. Johnny walks through the launderette and pauses at the door, looking out but allowing Omar to hold him from behind. There is no verbal resolution between them and typically the film denies us any articulated explanation for Johnny's change of mind. Instead, a cut to the final scene shows the two in long-shot at either side of the sink, splashing each other with water as the launderette bubble music comes up again. The future remains unresolved.

Narrative structures do not operate on their own and we shall explore further some of the issues raised in this analysis by looking at questions of narrative space and characterisation. But here I want to emphasise that the kind of analysis I have developed above can be misleading in smoothing over some of the discontinuities of the story. Although it is possible to piece together, as I have done, the narrative lines of *My Beautiful Laundrette*, the experience of watching the film is, at various points, one of narrative *discontinuities*. This is particularly true of the first part of the film up to the launderette opening. Thus, the first scene of Omar and Papa in the flat is not cut smoothly on actions but edited discontinuously, giving a slightly jumpy effect. At other points, the causal link between scenes is sometimes not clearly made: thus, it takes time for the opening scene to be explained by the arrival of Johnny into the story; the cut from Omar listening to Nasser and Rachel's lovemaking to the smart bar is explained only later on in the scene as it becomes clear that he is there at Nasser's invitation; the move from Omar claiming management of the launderette to seeking help from Salim is not explained by any narrative evidence of Omar's difficulties and is covered only by a high general shot of Johnny in the area. In addition, certain important moments are built up but then played down or avoided, as we have noted with the 'gangster' scenes of robbery and drug dealing. Typical is the handling of the crucial narrative event of Omar being given the launderette. The importance of this is signalled by his first invitation to the house, when Nasser promises, 'I've got a big challenge lined up [for Omar].' We see Omar dressing up in preparation for the visit but, in the event, there is no formal discussion between Nasser and Omar at the house. Instead of being announced by Nasser, the news that Omar is to run the launderette is introduced through an offhand insult by Tania, is reinforced, in a joking manner, by Nasser, who pronounces that the 'gora Englishman' always needs 'clean clothes', and is then subjected to Papa's scorn when Omar returns home. Thus a key element in one of the central storylines is introduced in a tangential way and is immediately put into the different contexts that undermine Nasser's claims that it should be seen as a promising business challenge.

It is important to note, however, that these narrative discontinuities and elisions are differently handled in the two main stories. The business story, although it contains strange, rather discontinuous scenes, builds momentum as the film progresses and develops into a rise-and-fall narrative reminiscent of a gangster film. In the business plot, Omar is clearly the singular hero, the innocent who has to learn to be 'hard' and to look out for himself. He articulates his ambitions clearly and, as the film progresses, becomes more experienced and confident in his dealings with Salim and Zaki. Events in this plot are built up through fairly classic cause-and-effect links. Omar earns Nasser's approval for his efforts in car washing and accounts. He works up to the successful opening of the launderette by employing Johnny to clear the place out and by discovering and raiding Salim's drug activities. After the opening, Omar continues to live off his wits and operate as a successful businessman but this plot's rise-and-fall structure is provided by Salim's downfall. From the highlight of the launderette's opening, the film goes into a downward spiral, generated largely by Salim's actions. Salim demands his drug money back and Omar and Johnny carry out the robbery to get it, only to be told by Salim that this was 'an educational test' of initiative; Omar shows his initiative by taking on more launderettes and offering Salim a share in the business as cover for his more dubious activities; Salim, however, drives into the gang and thereby brings to a head Johnny's simmering antagonism and directly triggers the gang's attack on the launderette. Thus, the second half of the film gathers pace and menace through a series of linked narrative actions which lead to the climax of the fight and Salim's defeat.

This onward momentum, which drives the business plot in the second half of the film, is underpinned by a running commentary that relates these activities to the film's challenge to right-wing politics. The film presents the activities of Nasser and Salim ironically as references to unemployment, Thatcherism and racism intertwine in their dialogue. The pair view themselves as ideal entrepreneurs in 'this damn country', which Nasser hates for its racism and loves because in England 'you can get anything you want. It's all spread out and available.' Nasser wants to separate out race and moneymaking, telling Johnny that he is 'a professional businessman not a professional Pakistani' and criticising Pakistan as a country 'sodomized by religion' which has begun 'to interfere with the making of money'. Salim asserts that it is only money which protects Pakistanis in England and combats racial abuse by directly adopting its language. He tells Omar that giving him a job means 'you'll be with your own people. Not in the dole queue.' 'Mrs Thatcher will be pleased with me,' he adds, not just because he is saving the country unemployment benefits but also because he is using her language of belonging and exclusion. Salim describes Johnny's gang as 'filthy and ignorant', as 'nothing' and as 'scum', but, in a further irony, he shares this racist rhetoric with the gang members, who object to Johnny working for 'Pakis', accuse him, in an early application of the Tebbit sporting test, of not supporting England at football any more and warn him not to 'cut yourself off from your own people'.

The business plot thus has a clear structure, narrative events that work through cause and effect and a set of political themes based on ironic inversions. This political dimension also helps to position the secondary story of the two brothers, in which the contrast between them indicates the complexity of emigrant, diasporic experiences. Nasser tells Omar of his love for Papa but mocking references to his brother are a necessary feature of Nasser's self-esteem. Papa is Nasser's opposite, a man with status in Pakistan – 'Politicians sought him out. Bhutto was his close friend,' Salim tells Omar – who has failed to find a comparable role in Britain. Papa's mantra for life as an immigrant is education rather than money. Nasser's message that life in Britain can be built on an understanding of its economics is paralleled by Papa's insistence that only education can bring the knowledge needed 'in order to see clearly what is being done and to whom in this country'. Even when Nasser's losses drive him to seek out his brother, political divisions and a different understanding of where 'home' is still come between them and contribute to the film's political dimension.

In contrast, the story of the gay romance is much less clear cut and the effect of its narrative organisation is to make the whole film seem more tentative and less settled. The romance genre, as described by Radway and Schatz[4] among others, provides for stories in which the pre-destined couple overcome internal and external obstacles to be with each other and achieve a stable position in society. Such narratives start with two central characters who move into a position in which they act as one; thus, while there are problems on the way, the narrative drives to the resolution in which the integration of the couple into society provides a happy ending. The romance plot of *My Beautiful Laundrette* has the two central characters of the standard romance but moves much less surely to that final resolution. Its narrative proceeds not by the gradual creation of a couple but in a series of zigzags in which the two come together, move apart and come together again. Omar's aims in relation to Johnny are never quite clear and, though Johnny is more articulate in his desire, he too backs away from its implications.

The high spots of the romance plot are the points where Omar and Johnny's actions and desires connect. The first meeting between the pair is accidental, a crossing of paths generated by Omar's position in his family ('the chauffeur', Johnny mocks) and Johnny's in the gang; the scene ends with mutual desire to meet again but the movement towards each other is followed by separation as Omar turns down Johnny's offer that 'we can do something now. Just us.' Following generic conventions, Omar then seeks Johnny out and Johnny responds, but this initially results in a business relationship. While the business plot, in which Johnny operates as a helper rather than a partner, develops incrementally, the high points of the romance – the kiss in the dark street, the hug which Salim observes outside the launderette, the lovemaking at the launderette opening, the playful splashing in the final shot – are paralleled by narrative moments of failure or pulling back. Thus, the tryst in the open car under the moon is disturbed when Omar raises the question of Johnny's racist past and his treatment of Papa and the two separate for the night. 'Much good can come of fucking,' Omar tells his surprised family but the sex at the launderette is not the classic happy ending but, instead, is followed by separation as Omar continues to pay half-hearted court to Tania and Johnny rejoins the gang. The next scene illustrates the pattern of one lover seeking to move the affair forward as the other moves away. Omar seeks Johnny out at a noisy party that serves to underline his isolation. At first, it appears that Omar is pursuing Johnny, who rejects him, telling him 'you're greedy'. Omar then insists on their contractual relationship, threatening that 'you're fired' unless he gets back to work. Johnny then tries to pick up on their personal relationship but this time Omar turns him down, saying that he's 'got some big thinking to do'. Johnny reminds him that 'it's been the best day', but Omar, looking away from him offscreen, corrects him – 'almost the best day'. The two go their separate ways again and the relationship is next picked up, apparently for business reasons, when Omar needs help from Johnny to repay Salim's money. The two continue to move towards and away from each other, in this way, as the business plot reaches its dénouement. After Salim's defeat and the gang members' flight, the pair are left without their other alliances. But even in the final scene the conventionally happy ending of the romance is precarious as Johnny initially makes a move to go, standing at the door looking away from Omar just as Omar had done earlier in Johnny's room.

A further element in the romance is the role of Tania as the third element in a 'romantic' triangle. This pattern is pre-figured when Johnny picks up a girl whom Omar had commented on admiringly in the club. Both Omar and Johnny attempt to use Tania for their own ends. Omar tries to cement his relations with Nasser by responding to the demand that he marry her; Omar never actually refuses this possibility – 'can't really get out if it', he tells Johnny – until Tania forcefully solves the problem by rejecting him. Johnny also uses Tania, in particular to get back at Omar and his family at Nasser's party. Johnny, like Tania, refuses the role assigned to him by the family – 'take charge of the music for us', Cherry orders him; instead he and Tania join forces first to mock and then to break up the party. But the alliance proves temporary and Johnny leaves with Omar, ignoring Tania's plea of 'take me'. Ironically, it is to Tania that Johnny makes his most articulate commitment about the absent Omar, refusing to react to the suggestion that Omar sees him only as an employee, 'a servant', and insisting 'I'll stay here with my friend and fight it out'.

It is possible to fill in the gaps and absences in this romance plot; Omar's anger at Johnny's past treatment of his father and Johnny's disapproval of Salim both figure in these comings and goings, but the pair never fully work through these feelings. The relationship's ambivalent commitments and joyous sexuality may also be based on a desire to allow this gay relationship to slip round the conventions of the traditional romance plot. It is striking, however, that compared to the business plot there is no meta-commentary that positions this relationship within a political discourse. While Omar's entrepreneurial ambitions are positioned in a recognisably Thatcherite economy, Omar and Johnny's relationship is developed outside the debates about gay rights and sexual orientation that were a feature of left-wing eighties politics. It is this refusal which singles out the romance plot and which was indeed welcomed by gay critics; no ideological justification is offered for actions that the characters themselves do not explain. The gay romance plot therefore offers the pleasures of the romance narrative but refuses to pin the couple down or to define them by the ideal moment of romantic fulfilment. In refusing explicit statements or political connections, the gay romance provides a counterpoint to the more explicit causal links and political commentary of the business plot.

NARRATIVE SPACE AND *MISE-EN-SCÈNE*

This analysis of the film's narrative organisation reveals that it is a complex form in which the narrative drive is diffused across a number of stories and is subject to discontinuities and red herrings. It demonstrates that the two central plots work rather differently in terms of how they organise the central characters and themes. If *Laundrette* is not exactly an example of television drama showing the 'wonderfully quiet knowledge about the intricacies of human motivation',[5] which Mark Le Fanu thought was the role of television, it does perhaps have television's interweaving plot lines and what some critics saw as an excess of the social problems of race, class and gender that British television drama drew on for subject matter. But to this analysis of the film's narrative structure we now need to add a discussion of the film's *mise-en-scène*, and in particular its use of narrative space. By this, I mean the way in which setting, camera and lighting work to create particular spaces that operate symbolically and which structure the way in which particular narrative events are experienced. One of the odd things about *My Beautiful Laundrette* is that what is rather a bleak story about the apparent failure of a business enterprise and the fragility of a relationship should have been welcomed as hopeful and uplifting. The answer to this lies in the way in which utopian possibilities are presented through the organisation of film space.

Its opening indicates that this is a film which is calling on the realist traditions most closely associated with Stephen Frears's mentors on British television, in particular Ken Loach and Tony Garnett. A recognisable situation (the clearing of the squat) with political and social implications (homelessness, the disaffection of youth) is given dramatic resonance by hand-held camerawork, strong close-ups, natural lighting and an authentic location. The dialogue is pared down, largely delivered in South London accents, and the audience is positioned inside the squat with the socially deprived. In the manner of social realism, a national problem is indicated but treated in such a way as to emphasise its lived particularity. *My Beautiful Laundrette* could certainly have continued in this way but the credits, with their flat row of pastel machines strung out across the middle of the screen, perhaps indicate that something different will occur. In fact, the realist mode is used throughout the film, particularly in scenes of violence such as the 'unscrewing' of Nasser's tenants and the fight at the end. The latter scene is filmed with graphic naturalism, the camera in close to record Salim's head smashed on the car bonnet and the intimate grappling of Genghis and Johnny. But in the rest of the film this realist approach is transformed into something more symbolic, an approach that expressively dramatises the threats and possibilities of the society in which Johnny and Omar live.

This works through a *mise-en-scène* that is considerably more complex than might first appear. It deploys a series of spatial distinctions between the streets and interiors and within the main sets, as well as the use of distinctive camerawork, lighting and character positioning. The first distinction is between the streets and interiors. After the pre-credits scene in the garden, there are two main sources of exterior settings – the streets of the gang and the area outside the launderette. The streets of the gang are clearly marked as threatening; they are not specifically located but become a general view of urban hell with the red of the traffic light as a warning sign. In the first incident, the arches of the viaduct create the impression of being in an underworld. A red glow and strong white flashes of light illuminate the distorted faces and bodies viewed from inside the car. When Omar moves out of the car to Johnny, the gang members remain in the red light while white light, reflecting on a background of white tiles, floods Johnny's face and Omar, in close-up, is lit by a warmer orange. Johnny's isolation and separation from the incident and from Omar are marked by a white fence running across the screen, and as the gang members move away from the car they throw strong shadows against the indeterminate arches of the viaduct. In the second incident, when Salim deliberately drives at the gang, the space becomes even more abstract, the gang members appearing as shadowy figures against misty blue light as they bang on the roof of a passing car. Members of the gang are specifically identified only after Salim's attack when the shadow of the car moves across the arches and blue and yellow light distorts Genghis's features in a close-up which indicates that he has identified the perpetrators.

The street outside the launderette also takes on a threatening aspect but this is achieved rather differently. Often filmed in a naturalist daylight, the street is nevertheless shot in such a way as to give it the appearance of a flat cinematic set, resembling in particular the main street in a Western. This is a space for watching and observing: Salim watches Johnny decorating and Omar hugging him from here and later puzzles that 'there's some things between them I'm looking into'; the extended dénouement begins with glimpses of the gang members positioning themselves on the roof and in the street, watching for the opportunity to attack. The street is also the place where fights break out. The argument between Nasser and Rachel, after the launderette opening, is filmed in long-shot here with the two facing each other like Western protagonists. Salim takes Omar into the street to lecture him about the importance of money while Johnny defiantly rejoins the gang, hanging around outside. And of course the attack on Salim's car parked outside the launderette kicks off a prolonged fight in the street with Genghis leaping down from the roof like a villain in a Western to join in. The dustbin through the window marks the end of the fight but also indicates a breaching of the boundary between exterior and interior. The violence of the street breaks through into the launderette.

The dangers of the night-time streets can, however, be transformed into sexual excitement and romance. This involves a complexifying of the space, making it less abstract and less flat, and is often reinforced by the use of music. In the scene under the bridge, music issues a warning as the car stops and it starts up again as Johnny is revealed. Magical chords accompany Omar as he walks into the threatening space to make contact with him by shaking hands across the dividing

5. *Johnny against the flat corrugated iron on the street.* (*Source*: BFI Collections, courtesy of FilmFour)

fence. Later on, outside the launderette but in a different space, Omar
and Johnny walk down-screen towards the main street, weaving past
a bollard before they reach the dark corner where Johnny pulls Omar

into their first kiss. The kiss is broken by noises, however, and Johnny looks round the corner along the shopfronts (thus turning the street into a flat space again) to see the silhouettes of the gang members outside the launderette. A scene with a similar combination of sexual excitement and threat follows immediately. In a dark street, lit by an idyllic and highly conventional moon, and accompanied by music, Omar and Johnny are kissing in the open-top car. But as they part, Johnny returns to possess the derelict streets again, caught in a flat tracking shot as he lopes past the backdrop provided by the abstract red-and-green graffiti on the corrugated iron that surrounds a squat.

Although the streets are constructed as urban spaces that are dangerous and unpredictable, the film does not make a simple division between the danger of the exteriors and the safety of the interiors. The interiors may offer some protection but the film indicates that they are complex places, offering secret spaces in which shifting relationships are presented. We can see how this is organised with increasing complexity in various settings in the film. The first and in some ways most straightforward internal space is the garage. Omar enters this space by walking down the slope out of the natural light into the parking area; this is indeed the last time we will see him in daylight until Nasser takes him to see the launderette. Within the garage are what appear to be two further spaces, the garage office and its back room. These spaces are differently used and controlled. The parking area is the potentially permeable space between the streets and the business; Salim takes Omar for an intruder there and Johnny comes into it unchallenged until he presses his face against the office window. The office is the public space of the men of the business, dominated by Nasser and a poster of *Some Like It Hot*, but accessible to those tied together by the business interests. Nasser and Salim are initially found in it and Omar gains access to it through his work; Nasser's invitation to help with the accounts is followed by a shot of Omar in the office working at the desk. Rachel walks confidently through the parking area but is not seen in the office. The back room is her area, seen only once but powerfully represented as the scene of laughter and sensuous lovemaking as the camera moves to reveal Rachel's body drenched in red light. Omar is excluded from this space; unlike many other doors in *My Beautiful Laundrette*, this door remains firmly closed as he eavesdrops from the other side.

Papa's flat is also constructed out of different spaces – a dark hall that leads on to the living room that is also Papa's bedroom, a kitchen area from which Papa's bed can be seen and, beyond the windows, a balcony that looks out on to the rail tracks and platform. These spaces are much more open to each other than the rooms in the garage and allow for more fluid movement between the characters. The bed is Papa's space and he dominates and directs Omar's action from it; Omar, by contrast, conducts his chores from the peripheries, washing and cooking around his father. But the closer Omar gets to the bed, the more intimate his acts of caring become and the more fiercely combative the relationship appears. Thus, one of the few occasions when Omar expresses anger with his father is when, kneeling by the bed, he responds to Papa's 'Illustrate your washing methods' by throwing the proffered laundry away. The bed is also the site of the extraordinary toe-nail-cutting scene, which starts with a huge close-up of Papa's foot being held by Omar. The two wrestle over the telephone as well as the foot and the excitement and troublesomeness of Johnny's call to re-establish contact seem to find expression in the intimacy and danger generated in the twists and kicks of Omar's physical care of his father. The bed is also the site of Nasser's weeping when he, the only visitor to the flat, finds Papa apparently lifeless on it. Nasser cries as he clutches him, the lowest point of his grief and the moment of greatest intimacy with his brother when he admits his own failures.

The balcony of the flat, on the other hand, is where distance and isolation are expressed. Omar tells Johnny that his mother jumped on to the railway line and perhaps she did it from here, a possibility that even more than the continual sounds of trains brings to mind *Brief Encounter* (Lean, 1945). Certainly Omar is frightened to find his father there at night when he returns from his first encounter with Johnny, the music that had accompanied him up the stairs to the hallway stopping as Omar discovers the empty bed and Papa outside in the bluish light. After the moonlit tryst with Johnny, Omar himself goes to the balcony in the same blue light and throws Papa's vodka bottle out, up on to the railway. And the moment of intimacy between Nasser and Papa at the end of the film is broken when they move on to the balcony; Nasser tries to reassure himself that everything will be all right, that Tania will marry Omar, only to see Tania unreachable on the platform. In the moment when Tania vanishes, so too does Papa back into the flat, leaving Nasser alone on the balcony. Given how the flat provides both a prison and a retreat for his father, it is perhaps not surprising that Omar delights in imagining him in different spaces – 'Tell me about the beach at Bombay, Uncle ... or the house in Lahore ... [when] Papa's bed started to float.'

6. *Nasser's bedroom, the male space in the house, with Nasser and Salim on the right.* (*Source*: BFI Collections, courtesy of FilmFour)

The flat and the garage are relatively closed spaces which few enter. Nasser's house, on the other hand, is open to many but is also organised around identifiable spaces. The drive, which often provides an establishing shot for scenes in the house, imposes Nasser's status on those who enter. Johnny waits here for Omar to call him in and, when they drive up for the party, the lights, cars and party atmosphere cause Johnny to mock 'this big Gatsby geezer' but also to reflect that 'perhaps this ain't my world'. Initially, inside the house, the emphasis is on separation. On Omar's first visit, we see him being introduced to the women of the family in a large room with bright lamps and pastel walls. Tania, in a movement befitting her rebellious state, then leads him from this female room to the male area but at this stage does not enter Nasser's room herself. Instead Omar tentatively pushes at the dark door so that the edge of its opening makes a cinematic wipe, gradually revealing the reclining Nasser surrounded by his cronies. Omar joins the men in this room, which is decorated with darker wood, panels and hangings, but outside Tania reappears at the silvery windows, baring her breasts to distract Omar from male conversations.

This room continues to be a male place where Nasser combines business with conviviality; his daughters are allowed in to pamper him with massages but Tania is expelled again when Johnny is invited in for the 'interview' that leads to him working for Nasser. But Nasser's house also contains a liminal space, the veranda, which, with its glass windows overlooking the garden, seems to hover between inside and outside. This is a secret place, but one that can be overlooked, a place where scandalous activity can be both indulged in and observed, a place where disruptive elements come together and part. On the veranda, on his first visit, Tania attempts to seduce Omar into helping her, taunts him about the launderette and asks him, as her mother stands outside the glass, about her father's 'mistress'. Omar and Johnny watch Bilquis, on the veranda, preparing her potions to use against Rachel, a scene interrupted first by Nasser storming in and then by Tania storming out, all under the gaze of the two young men. Finally, the veranda is the place where Nasser's party breaks up and the business and family relations that have given him status break down. From the veranda, Salim and Omar discuss business while watching Johnny and Tania cycle slowly round in the blue light of the garden, like some modern version of Robert Redford and Katharine Ross in *Butch Cassidy and the Sundance Kid* (Hill, 1969). By breaching the boundaries and riding the bike from the garden into the veranda, Johnny causes chaos, pushing Omar and Salim to the ground and bringing Nasser on to the scene. An angry Salim reveals that Nasser's business is in trouble while Tania, transgressively, again refers to Rachel and announces that she is leaving home.

These complex settings all demand cinematographic approaches that are themselves more complex than those envisaged in the essentialist view of television aesthetics outlined in Chapter 1. In particular, important activity often takes place in the background of a shot and light, reflections and shadows are used atmospherically to make space fluid. Omar's move into the office space in the garage, for instance, is marked by a shot of his dark head framed against the window through which in the deep background we can see the dazzling lights of Nasser's car. A continuous camera movement takes us through a wall and, as the car slowly drives into the foreground, Omar moves from the office into the parking area, amused and pleased by Nasser's orders to 'kiss Rachel'. Omar's change of status at work and in his relationships is thus expressed visually while the dark shadows and blue lighting give the scene a magical effect. Similarly, the brisk cutting and daylit ordinariness of Papa's flat give way to night-time scenes in which long-shots look from the dark hall through the living room to figures silhouetted on the balcony; the harsh, flickering light and the sounds of passing trains emphasise how the space is dominated by the railway. And the glass of the veranda at night reflects the fairy lights, the rain and the shadows from the garden, throwing a silvery, blurred illumination across the faces and bodies inside. In these cases, the visual organisation not only delineates the spaces and the interactions that will take place in them but transforms them into something different, a cinematic form of magic.

But it is of course the launderette which provides the most complex space and the most magical transformation. The launderette consists of a number of interlocking areas. First of all there is the pavement outside, part of the dangerous street but also linked to the launderette and visible from the inside through the plate-glass windows. Then there is the washing machine area, available to the general public for a variety of activities including, but not exclusively, washing clothes. Farther back is the office/storage area with a sink which is connected to the other areas by a door into the main area and, at the back, a window and a door that provides the back entrance.[6]

Unlike those of the garage, flat or house, the transformation of the launderette's setting is written into the film's narrative. Initially, it is organised so that the back office is visible from the main area, which itself is divided by the washing machines, which are placed at a right angle to the door and run across the screen. We see this early on when Salim enters the launderette in a shot that features a tiny insert of Omar in the background, visible through the open office door. This public space is dominated by the washing machines. They are a barrier that Salim has to walk round (we see only his shadow) and Johnny hop over; when Omar offers Johnny a job doing 'a variety of menial things', he sits on a machine at one end while Johnny walks round to the end of the line. In this spatial organisation, the main area belongs to members of the public, who have free run of the place. As in the garage, the office is a site for business. On his first visit, Salim closes the door and orders Omar to stand so that their faces are shadowy as the strong light is directed on to the desk at the bottom of the frame. When Salim returns for the second job, he takes Omar from the public area into the office and again shuts the door; this time, though, Omar reopens it and Johnny lounges in the doorway, his body positioned in the shot between Salim and Omar as Salim makes his proposal. Johnny finally enters the office when Omar takes him in there to discuss selling the drugs and thus brings him into the 'management' of the business.

The transformed launderette is differently arranged. The machines are now lined up against the brightly painted walls, leaving a public space that can be used fluidly in the middle. Blue and yellow motifs dominate the colour scheme and a large mirror provides reflections of the colours and movement while below it an aquarium of exotic fish bubbles away. The mirror also acts as a window which from inside connects the transformed office to what is going on outside. The office still contains the accoutrements of the business, a sink and cleaning equipment as well as a desk and chair, but the beaded curtains, mirror and blinds cast shadows and make it into a more intimate, private space.

The work of transformation is carried out by Johnny, whom we see smashing up the fixed line of washing machines and claiming the pavement outside with his ladders and painting gear. Our view of the inside of the launderette during this process is often obscured by white paint over the windows which provides an eerie reflection at night. Crucial to how we understand the transformation of the launderette is the scene the evening before the opening. In the dark street, a high camera at a side angle to the shopfront follows Johnny as he comes down from the ladder. Omar is fretting about Salim and business so he leaves the scene, but Johnny continues with the work, roping a gang member in to help him. The camera position now shows the front of the building, which fills the screen, and it moves with Johnny and Moose up the ladders, as they position the 'laundrette' sign. The camera is now higher than the protagonists, offering a view of the whole façade, which we have not seen before, in a shot that has no character source nor any narrative function except to show the spectacle of the neon lights. The blue lights of POWDERS light up across the screen and the neon washing powder pours into blue lines of water. In the published script, this scene concentrates more on Moose's panic at being caught helping, ending with a look between him and Genghis. In the film, Moose carries on up the ladder and the gang relationships take second place to the transformation created by the upward camera movement, the blue, pink and white lights and the chord of music that marks the completion. What is being offered directly to the audience, then, as a moment of magic, is the achievement of cinema in making an imaginative transformation of mundane reality. The unmotivated camera movement is offered by cinema itself, and what is revealed is not so much the transformed launderette as the dream palace of an old-fashioned cinema, its wares traced out in the neon that lights up the dark, dangerous street.

Initially it seems clear that what has been created is a utopian space. In a film full of references, perhaps it is appropriate to think of

Ealing's *Passport to Pimlico* (1949), in which a part of London briefly became a different country and a motley group of characters threw off government restrictions and social hierarchies. *My Beautiful Laundrette* is more cautious but perhaps in the end braver about what can happen. We saw in the narrative analysis how the various storylines came together in this long scene; now I want to explore how space is used to underpin this.

First, the office is taken over for romance as Omar and Johnny retreat there, initially for Omar to explain his feelings about Johnny's political betrayal and then for Johnny's seduction of Omar. The sexual activity of the pair, although taking place in the secret site of the office, is integrated into the public space of the launderette through the window; a single shot gives us Johnny and Omar naked and embracing in the foreground while Nasser and Rachel claim the public space in the background, dancing to the music of Strauss's *Wiener Blut* waltz, which swells on to the soundtrack. The soundtrack serves to bring the space outside the launderette into the scene as muted laughter and cheers from the waiting crowd can be heard behind the music. Two unlikely and transgressive relationships achieve their most fulfilled moments in a utopian, social context.

The space is then transformed as Nasser enters the office searching for Omar and Johnny and the crowd surges past the fragile barrier of the now-cut ribbon. The music changes to Copland's 'Fanfare for the Common Man', and from inside the office we see Johnny in the public space turn triumphantly to look at the hidden Omar, his face aligned with the reflection of his lover's face. Business and romance are brought into line through this spatial metaphor. A dissolve transforms the scene to a party in full swing, the public space now bustling, though Omar, still waiting for Papa, is caught looking out of frame through the windows. Gradually two sides begin to form: on the one, Omar and Nasser talk expansion while on the other the two white working-class figures, Rachel and Johnny, are grouped – 'I knew your mother,' Rachel tells him. Disruption is hinted at as Salim enters and members of the gang move across the screen. Tania's arrival, framed in the door, confirms the threat from the street outside and her movement into the launderette to join Rachel and Johnny disrupts the balance. Omar is sent over to prise her away, but Nasser and Rachel are effectively expelled by Tania's arrival and go out into the street to quarrel.

The long day continues, but now the space of the launderette is reconstituted down a vertical line. A number of long-shots show that the good-natured crowds have been replaced by the gang members at the back taunting Johnny, who in the middle ground is putting clothes in a machine while Salim sits near by. Tania and Omar are in the foreground by the door, discussing marriage. Omar and Johnny are no longer aligned and Tania and Salim are able to come between them. As we have seen, the final disintegration of the celebrations takes place out in the street but the scene closes with Omar back in the launderette. He peers through the mirror into the office, looking for Johnny, and walks round the nearly empty launderette to the door, where he looks out, offscreen, and shouts for him. In some ways this is puzzling since Omar has seen Johnny leave and would surely have seen him return had he done so. But it makes sense symbolically since the empty launderette and Johnny's absence demonstrate the fragility of the social activity that has been generated earlier in the utopian space of the launderette and of the film.

My Beautiful Laundrette's complex use of narrative space goes beyond the process of giving a realistic setting for the plot and characters or providing naturalistic evidence for the exploration of social problems. The manipulation of narrative space described here has the effect of transforming mundane settings into symbolic locations and, in particular, rendering the romance plot both more coherent and more utopian because it is centred on the launderette. This is not just a question of the organisation of space through setting. The relationship between Omar and Johnny is also built up through a series of shots in which it is the space between the pair which expresses sexual excitement. The first of these occurs as Johnny, who has been waiting in the drive, is brought into Nasser's house: in the liminal space of the doorway, two brief shots catch Johnny's head moving back as Omar brushes his cheek and a close-up of a smiling Omar; the final shot of the scene frames Omar and Johnny in the doorway, both looking towards Tania in the space between them as Johnny pulls the door shut into a fade. The sex scene in the launderette office shows Omar and Johnny alone, and just before they kiss their two heads are again framed, more tightly this time, on either side of the screen; darkness blots out Omar as Johnny turns off the light and the gap between them disappears as they kiss. But, as Rachel and Nasser leave the launderette opening, Tania is reinserted into the relationship; Omar and Johnny are positioned side by side looking at each other and then at Tania while she, on the left of the screen, watches her father and his mistress leave. In another such shot, Johnny and Omar are brought together again visually at Nasser's house after their temporary

7. *Rachel and Nasser as they say goodbye, characteristically shot through
the bar grille.* (*Source*: BFI Collections, courtesy of FilmFour)

separation. Their heads, facing each other on either side of the image,
frame Bilquis and Tania on the veranda. 'We have to do a job ... Just
to get us through,' says Johnny. 'You want that, don't you?' 'Yes,' says
Omar, changing the object and the meaning, 'I want you.' The ending
again expresses their relationship spatially through a long-shot of them
facing each other and splashing water from the sink between them, the
space between this time filled by a mirror which reflects only Omar.
Although narratively the relationship may be unstable, the repetition of
this visual figure gives a hint that somewhere, in the imaginary spaces
of the launderette, it may continue.

In addition to this visual rendering of the characters' emotional and
moral positions, the film consistently makes use of and draws attention
to a visual register that brings together camera movement, lighting and
setting to generate a pleasure beyond that of following the story. The
film's *mise-en-scène* is marked by shots that emphasise the fact of viewing, as if we are catching a revelatory moment of action which may
soon be withdrawn. Shadows and barriers come between the viewer and
the full action. Thus, the scene of Rachel and Nasser's lovemaking is
filmed in dim, red light as the camera moves behind what appear to be
empty wine racks, while the scene of their parting, again in muted red
light, is filmed through the squares of a black grille. In the launderette

office, as Omar talks about his father, shadows from the bead curtain fall across his face.

Throughout the film, mirrors, glass and windows both allow us to see the action and slightly obscure it. Omar's animated face is caught in a mirror while his father mocks his excitement about 'scrubbing cars', and Omar gets a glimpse of Salim's drug carrier in the mirror of the anonymous hotel room. Salim, Omar and Johnny all use or are observed in car mirrors, and the first shot of a car often allows the driver to be viewed initially only through the glass of the windscreen. The glass of the launderette windows sometimes forces the audience to observe action inside as if it were under water, actions slightly blurred and with muted sound. Thus, Omar's excitement when he rushes into the launderette with the beard is muted by the glass, and we see but do not hear what is going on when Johnny returns to deal with the odd customers who remain on the opening night. Sometimes the audience penetrates the mirror or glass, as for instance in the joyous moment when we cut from Salim's view of Omar and Johnny in his car mirror to Johnny's secret lick of Omar's neck provided by a close shot and a different angle. Sometimes, though, the transparent barrier continues to be effective. In the final scene, the gang's attack on the car is observed in a tracking shot across the window from the inside of the launderette while, as the fight begins, in the reverse position, we are distanced from Johnny's emotions and motivations, observing him in long-shot from outside as he watches the onslaught in the street from behind the window.

Doors too create an ambivalent viewing position. Pushed open, they can reveal activity which the act of eavesdropping makes intriguing and perhaps suspicious: Nasser's manly jokes about Papa; Bilquis watching her guests' departure after overhearing Tania's questions about Rachel; Salim's smooth boasting at his dinner party. But doors that are opened can also be closed: Salim, framed in the doorway and caught in the mirror as he inspects the beard, shoves the door shut against Omar and the audience; after Rachel leaves, the swinging doors move on empty air, indicating the felt presence of her absence from Nasser's life; Johnny shuts the door on the audience for a moment as he first enters Nasser's house. And the final shot of the film is the door being closed, this time by an unseen hand, on the image of Omar and Johnny at the sink. Action continues but the invitation to this private place is being withdrawn.

The door closing can be understood as a reference to the act of film-making, which has now been completed. Other shots seem also to revel in drawing attention to the act of film-making or presenting unexpected aesthetic pleasures. Thus, *My Beautiful Laundrette* uses a variety of camera angles, employing a repertoire that is rather different from the medium shots or close-ups often associated with television. Establishing shots are frequently from odd angles, low angles, for instance, often being employed around the cars, while high-angle shots punctuate the narrative at various points. Complex shot compositions put important actions or characters in the background while, in an apparently more straightforward framing, a striking mural demands attention during a politically charged piece of dialogue. In addition, the film also features what are, in this context, quite bravura shots, drawing attention to camera movement. Before the fist meeting with the gang, the camera records a train rattling across the viaduct before dropping to the arches below to discover Salim's car waiting at the red light. The disco scene when Johnny sells the drugs is filmed in one shot which pans and tracks from Omar at one end of the room, past Johnny doing his deal, picks up Omar again and then discovers Johnny dancing at the other end of the bar. When Johnny angrily abandons Omar at Zaki's launderette, a high shot picks up the car driving off; when he arrives at 'Powders', the camera records him entering at the back of the building and then moves upward and across the flat roof before coming down into the street on the other side at the front of the building, thus showing how the gang is gathering. Such camerawork always makes a narrative point but does so in a way that draws attention to the ability of cinema to provide spectacular effects, even in the context of a low-budget television film.

My Beautiful Laundrette is a film that is suffused with visual flourishes and framings, and there are thus indications of a move away from the naturalism of its opening to a style in which the image becomes what John Caughie calls 'an aesthetic object for contemplation'.[7] Christopher Williams suggests that many Film on Four films between 1982 and 1991 pursued this route, finding that the 'art film' constitutes the largest single category.[8] In this kind of work, the style of the film is a source of aesthetic pleasure and is linked to themes of alienation, ambiguity and individual subjectivity. But although *My Beautiful Laundrette* does have a distinctive visual style, it is used to different ends. Style is always linked to narrative so that contemplation of the aesthetic effects is still accompanied by specific narrative action. Nevertheless, the visual effects go beyond Simon Perry's notion of television as a 'purveyor of illustrated information'.[9] We saw earlier how the presentation of the transformed launderette was strongly aligned with the magical powers of cinema. I would suggest that, throughout the film, the *mise-en-scène* works to sustain this sense of cinema as a place for the unexpected, whether it be the swoop of a camera right over a building, the editing that allows Tania to disappear, the lighting that, with its blue, reds and oranges, transforms the urban settings into symbolic spaces, or the windows, mirrors and doors that control what can and cannot be seen. Such a *mise-en-scène* works not at the level of contemplation and ambiguity but in the context of engagement and surprise, an effect reinforced by the magical chords of the electronic music. This surely helps to explain the way in which critics praised the film for its pleasures as well as its political significance, describing it as entertaining, zany, fresh and quirky. The film's visual discourse serves a double function. The imaginative pleasures of popular cinema are transferred to the stories of racial and sexual politics, appropriate and challenging in 1980s Britain. But, in addition, this film, with its serious political and social intentions, becomes a celebration of cinema itself as a utopian space, a site of transforming and life-enhancing activity. The call for cinematic release was evidently appropriate.

ACTING AND PERFORMANCE

One of the pleasures of British cinema is frequently deemed to be strong acting performances. While Hollywood seeks to attract audiences through the establishment and maintenance of stars, British films regularly draw on actors and actresses who have a theatrical pedigree, and the ability to act is claimed as a key difference between British and Hollywood stars. Associations between acting and quality characterised the critical success of the heritage film in the 1980s. As John Hill suggests, the genre's emphasis on display and spectacle 'also extends to the demonstration of a certain theatricality, involving "quality" actors often more commonly associated with the stage'.[10] Such acting involves a 'clear display of "actorliness"' through 'overtly theatrical performances which clearly announce their status as performance' (p. 82). In addition, the narratives of such films focus on a group of characters, with the emphasis on 'characterisation and conversational exchange' (p. 80), and thus encourage ensemble playing and cameo roles rather than domination by one or two stars. The full-blown characteristics of the genre were perhaps not fully established in 1985; *Room with a View* was released, as we have seen, in 1986, a few months after *Laundrette*, and *Howards End* did not appear until 1991. But *Chariots of Fire*, *Heat and Dust* (1982) and *Passage to India* (1984) had shown the way, while on television two Granada productions, *Brideshead Revisited* (1981) and *The Jewel in the Crown* (1984), had won critical acclaim and overseas sales by similarly providing a showcase for great British actors in adaptations set in the past. Frears was perhaps thinking of such performances when, in a 1989 interview, he commented that 'British actors are very good about playing manners' but that the consequence could be turning a film into 'something behind glass'.[11]

Film on Four supported such productions, and indeed had a financial stake in *Heat and Dust* and *A Room with a View*, but *My Beautiful Laundrette* was defiantly different. Kureishi's anger with the Raj films, the 'Easterns', was an impetus for his own script.[12] Nevertheless, the quality of acting was, for many critics, a measure to be applied to *My Beautiful Laundrette*. What is striking indeed in looking at the reviews is both how often acting is mentioned and what a wide range of actors in the film are commended for their performances. Although David Castell commented that the acting 'seems to me to range from the stilted to the downright wooden',[13] most other critics found much to commend. For some, 'the youthful performances of Gordon Warnecke, Daniel Day Lewis and Rita Wolf', were at the heart of the film with Derek Malcolm suggesting that 'no more convincing examples of eighties youth exist on the screen at the moment'.[14] *The Spectator* argued that 'comedy ... depends on the instinctive skill of its performers' and suggested that 'even in this the film was well served' by Warnecke and Day-Lewis.[15] Day Lewis received particular praise from a number of critics, including the *London Standard* and *Girl about Town*. Others picked out Roshan Seth and particularly Saeed Jaffrey; *New Socialist* welcomed the fact that they had been allowed to escape from 'a string of trivial bit-parts' while *The Listener* singled out the 'marvellous performances' of the pair.[16] Shirley Ann Field's 'glamorous ageing mistress' was praised as 'exquisitely observed'.[17] In some cases, a number of cast members get mentioned with Iain Johnstone being particularly enthusiastic, commenting that Jaffrey and Seth 'once again demonstrate what superb actors they are, Gordon Warnecke manages the maturing of Omar with conviction and Daniel Day Lewis contrives to be emotionally honest and politically rebarbative as Johnny'.[18] These kinds of review illustrate that *My Beautiful Laundrette* fits the critical criteria applied to the very different heritage films; acting is used as a measure of distinctive quality and the emphasis is on the range of performances provided by a number of actors, rather than on the outstanding appearance of a star.

This emphasis on fine performances throughout the cast was also important for the US reviews. *Variety*, in its report on the Edinburgh screening, commented on 'a gallery of fine performances', including 'standout performances' from Jaffrey and Field.[19] Reporting on the film again, just before its opening in the USA, it points to 'a fine cast', including 'two internationally known Indian actors' and 'young talents' in Warnecke and Day-Lewis.[20] Andrew Sarris praised the acting as 'uniformly good' while Vincent Canby commended Day-Lewis for a performance that has 'both extraordinary technical flash and emotional substance', Warnecke for being 'wonderfully insidious as Omar' and mentioned Jaffrey and Seth as being 'fine'.[21] Pauline Kael unusually comments that 'the visual presence of the women characters is so strong that we get a sense of what their lives are' and gives a particular nod to Rita Wolf, 'who becomes more attractive and impressive with each appearance'.[22]

This sustained commentary on acting indicates an area worth exploring. What is particularly interesting about the performances in *My Beautiful Laundrette*, however, as compared perhaps with some of the heritage films, is that they are very varied. Actors in the film are at different stages of their careers, bring very different sets of connotations to their roles and are working in different traditions. Looking at some of the key performances, then, opens up again the unevenness and contradictory emphases of the film and also begins the process of reinserting the film back into a wider context, this time relating it to discourses of stardom and acting. In looking at some of the performances in the film, I shall accordingly take into account both textual and extra-textual factors.

As with their characters, Daniel Day-Lewis and Gordon Warnecke offer contrasting performances and personae. For both of them, *My Beautiful Laundrette* was a key moment in their careers and, as we have seen, their performances contributed to the film's success. But it is also clear that they were used differently and that their participation in the film had different effects on their careers. Of the two, Day-Lewis came to the film with much stronger acting experience. He had gone to drama school at the Bristol Old Vic, had appeared in successful West End productions in London and for the Royal Shakespeare Company (RSC). He had some film and television experience, including a large co-production, *The Bounty* (1984). He also had an unusual background which combined the bohemian and artistic with the conventions of the British Establishment. He was the grandson of Michael Balcon, the head of Ealing Studios in the 'golden age' of British cinema; his father, Cecil Day-Lewis, had been Poet Laureate and his mother was the British actress Jill Balcon. He grew up in south-east London, but in posh Greenwich rather than rough Lewisham, and went to boarding school in Sevenoaks, which he later described himself as hating, until a transfer to the more progressive Bedales.

All this background was grist to the publicity mill, and Day-Lewis's biography was used extensively in the interviews and profiles that accompanied the release of the film in Britain and the USA. Two stories dominate the developing star image. The first is that of his upbringing, which draws attention to the gap in class, appearance and attitudes between Day-Lewis and the character of Johnny. Day-Lewis tries to bridge the gap by claiming that, before going to boarding school, he had grown up in south-east London, "'quite close to where *Laundrette* is set'", that "'I went to a school in South London with kids just like Johnny'" and enjoyed holiday work loading lorries in Deptford.[23] Despite all this, Day-Lewis recognises that he had had to "'use a lot of camouflage to survive'" in Lewisham and Deptford as a boy and that the character's position is very different from his own.[24] This is implicit in the second story which features in the publicity, the tale of how Day-Lewis so badly wanted the part that he threatened Frears into giving it to him. Many profiles refer to this episode: "'Don't be fooled by my polite background," he wrote [to Frears], "I've got some very unpleasant friends." Frears gave him the part, confiding later that "I always think that if someone wants a part that badly, then they should have it."'[25]

In terms of acting traditions, Day-Lewis is described as admiring Montgomery Clift, James Dean and Marlon Brando, a list that indicates an interest in the Method approach, with its emphasis on the physical manifestation of internal trauma, made famous by these US stars; he emphasised that he did not want to become self-conscious about the process of acting: "'I always try to let the physicality of a character come from nowhere'".[26] But his list of favourites also included those working in the British tradition of the observed detail of a character, Anthony Hopkins and Alec Guinness. Richard Eyre, who directed him in a BBC television film, *The Insurance Man*, in 1985, and also as an ill-fated Hamlet at the National Theatre in 1989, thought that he was 'much more comfortable as a character actor, playing someone from whom he has a distance'.[27]

Day-Lewis's performance is one of the most remarkable aspects of the film, perhaps because it combines these two tendencies. It is character acting in the sense that Day-Lewis adopts the working-class speech and mannerisms of his character sufficiently well to handle the film's realist scenes. But the performance is also suffused with the physical glamour associated with stardom, identifiable in a number of ways. Firstly, Day-Lewis as Johnny is isolated from his surroundings and is set up to be looked at, by other characters and the audience. Thus, when Omar tells Nasser 'I've hired a bloke of outstanding strength', two flashbacks, the only ones in the film, show Johnny at work: the first, a high-angle shot, emphasises his chest and arms as he demolishes the machines, while in the second, a low-angle head-and-shoulder shot against the white ceiling, Day-Lewis looks and smiles at the camera. Such moments are often associated with conscious pleasure and satisfaction by Omar and others. When Johnny is introduced to Nasser and his business friends, they are grouped together on one side, while Johnny, in close-up, looks back at their eager faces. He is thus positioned so that he can be scrutinised by the family (and the viewer), Omar being with Salim and Nasser in the group of men, while Tania sits separately and closer but still facing Johnny until she is sent away. His face is slightly softened and the lighting and the blurred background of books emphasises Day-Lewis's strong features and his air of detached amusement. As in other scenes, Johnny's difference is reinforced by his casual dress; here, the soft grey top stands apart from the dark suits that Salim, Omar and the others are wearing.

The second way of marking Day-Lewis's performance as something different is the way in which he uses physical gesture and speech. Day-Lewis consistently 'presents' a gesture, drawing attention to the movement of his body as he does so. Thus, when Omar returns from Salim's errand with the beard, he is filmed running into the launderette; he touches Johnny and moves behind the machines, turning back to display the beard. His actions are joyous and excited but directed to moving the plot along. By contrast, Day-Lewis performs Johnny rather than the narrative, turning round once to look at Omar but then doing a second turn during which he throws clothes around his own back into the machine. It is a gesture of celebration, not just of Omar's excitement but of pleasure in the movement itself. Similarly, after he has licked Omar's neck, Day-Lewis turns round with a shimmy of his hips to Moose before he rushes away. And at Nasser's party, Johnny responds to the request that he take charge of the music with a dance gesture, hands above his head in parody. This gesture has a narrative function since Tania sees it and joins up with him to make trouble, but it also draws attention, as do other such gestures, to the way his body moves.

Day-Lewis similarly presents speech in an unusual way. He makes use of silences and brings a measured, drawling tone to his lines. Thus, in his first scene with Omar, Day-Lewis plays Johnny as observing his friend's eager approach and then turns his head from Omar's greeeting before ironically responding, 'I know who it is.' A similar pause in dialogue prefaces his slow drawl to Salim later in the film – 'in my experience, it's always worth waiting for Omo'. Delivering the line before the first kiss, Day-Lewis extends the word 'launderette' (ironically restoring the lost E) and rolls the Rs, declaiming 'a launderette as big as the Ritz', before seizing Omar. In gesture and voice, then, Day-Lewis emphasises performance, creating a distance between himself and his character in which irony can flourish.

Finally, Day-Lewis's performance is marked by enigma. As a character, he is the one of whom the most change is demanded as he shifts from skinhead leader to defender of a Pakistani lover. But although Omar, in particular, is given dialogue to reflect on this shift, Johnny is not; no speech gives us access to his political beliefs, neither does his face, its impassivity cracked only by an ironic smile. The commitment he makes most directly is a physical one to Omar, but any change of political views goes unarticulated even during his meeting with Papa. This lack of growth in his character feeds into the narrative discontinuities discussed earlier, but it also gives Day-Lewis's performance the kind of physical presence and iconic distance often associated with male stars. Indeed, this combination of character and performance is a reminder of an earlier figure who achieved stardom in his first film role – Albert Finney in *Saturday Night and Sunday Morning* (1960). Just as Finney's bodily presence imposed itself on a narratively weak character, so Day-Lewis's physical glamour overrides the political questions that the character raises.

This raises the question of whether Day-Lewis's performance affects the film's narrative, and I would suggest that it does. The star persona being established here fits the gay romance narrative well, depending as it does on the romance conventions of instant attraction and intuitive understanding of what lies behind silence. As we have seen, gesture can express motivation and carry the romance narrative forward, and touch provides the possibility of a happy ending. But the core of Day-Lewis's

Johnny, despite the character actor's attention to the detail of manners, is a cool acceptance of his own attractiveness. Played in this way, Johnny is too glamorous, intelligent and individual to be representative of the so-called Thatcherite underclass; he presents a self that is impervious to change and whose attraction lies in performance, not thought. In that sense, Day-Lewis's performance stretches the credibility of the story but adds immensely to the film's appeal.

This was evident as the dust began to settle and it was Day-Lewis who was picked out from the 'fine cast' for acting awards, in particular the New York Film Critics Circle award as best supporting actor in *My Beautiful Laundrette* and *A Room with a View*. This was particularly significant in terms of his subsequent career for, if the British press predicted 'the handsome Daniel's imminent transformation into a pin-up',[28] it was the American critics who confirmed it. The coincidence of his two films opening in New York on the same day provided the opportunity, as one headline put it, of comparing him 'playing a punk and a snob' and thus applauding him as 'one of the most versatile actors of his generation'.[29] Thus, despite the general commendations for the cast, it is Day-Lewis who is particularly picked out in language that indicates a burgeoning star. Kael's review ended with a reminder that in *The Bounty* he had 'stuck out' and 'seemed like a bad actor'. Here, though, his 'performance gives the movie an imaginative, seductive spark', and she describes the intelligence and danger of the role and the performance.[30] By May 1986 the theatre critic Nicholas de Jongh could describe Day-Lewis as 'suddenly, utterly modish'[31] and so he continued, giving an Oscar-winning performance in *My Left Foot* (1989) and confirming his star status in a physically demanding *The Last of the Mohicans* (1992).

If *My Beautiful Laundrette* was the launch pad for Day-Lewis, it was the high spot of Gordon Warnecke's career. In a discussion of *Sammy and Rosie Get Laid* (1987), Frears later commented on working with black or Asian actors: 'If you make a film with a lot of black or Asian actors, generally speaking they've had few opportunities to act. So there aren't many good English speaking Asian actors ... So you end up with someone quite inexperienced.'[32]

This was presumably the case with Warnecke, whose first film this was, though he had been to drama school and had some theatrical experience. Unlike with Day-Lewis, there seems to have been no usable hinterland for publicity and, considering his is the major role, Warnecke features in very little of the PR for the film. Nevertheless, the performance is skilful in the way in which it fleshes out Omar's character and shows how he develops and changes. In the early scenes, he communicates a naive freshness, his eager face turned towards his father and then his uncle as he seeks to make his way in the world. Close-ups here are more about character than bodily display and are often comical; hence, his grimace as Papa pinches his cheek and his gleeful smile as he eavesdrops on the lovemaking in the office. Warnecke's eyes move rapidly, expressing Omar's eagerness to take everything in; at times – for example, when he prepares to go to Nasser's house for the first time – he shines with excitement. Gradually, as the business plot develops, Warnecke shows Omar's growing confidence, and in his final scene with Zaki he is clearly in control, briskly leading the older man and snapping out the dialogue.

Warnecke's acting thus fits a realist approach that emphasises the character's motivation and sets his eagerness and naivety in opposition to Day-Lewis's more enigmatic approach. He is less convincing at other points, particularly when Omar seeks to dominate Johnny. In such situations, Omar's assertive dialogue is undermined by the way in which the visual register supports the power of Johnny's presence. Thus, on Johnny's first visit to the launderette, Warnecke's slight figure is dominated by the way Day-Lewis is framed in the front of the image and his verbal orders, given from a sitting position perched on a washing machine, are undercut by Day-Lewis's prowl round the premises. Similarly, Omar's admonishments to Johnny about returning to work after the opening carry less force than the non-verbal communication of strength in Johnny's shadowy face and exposed chest. In both cases, it is not so much that Warnecke lacks conviction or skill but that he is up against another kind of performance which is being supported, against the grain of the narrative, by the *mise-en-scène*.

Warnecke's performance did not make him a star. Indeed, it is possible to see his subsequent career as a demonstration of the problems facing black actors even after such a start. He appeared in two further films, Kureishi's *London Kills Me* (1991) and *The Pleasure Principle* (1991). Shortly after *Laundrette*, in 1986, he made television appearances in *Boon* and *Dr Who* and has continued such work, making appearances in popular programmes such as *The Bill* and taking a larger role in a Ruth Rendell adaptation, *A Fatal Inversion* (1992), alongside some work in the British soaps *EastEnders* and *Brookside*. He has undertaken theatrical work, including a small part with the RSC in 1988. But features on Warnecke tend to stress the fall after *Laundrette*: 'ever wonder what happened to Gordon Warnecke who played Omar in *My Beautiful Laundrette*?' asked the US *Trikone*, a magazine devoted to material of South Asian queer interest, while Warnecke has also featured in the more mainstream *Empire*'s 'Where are they now?' column.[33] Even allowing for differences in experience and quality of performance, the contrast in the subsequent careers of Warnecke and Day-Lewis is extreme. In a publicity interview at the time of his *Brookside* role, Warnecke expressed his frustration at the limitations placed on him: 'what I can't stand are narrow-minded people who think I can't do anything else other than play Asians'.[34]

Rita Wolf was also relatively inexperienced, though she had appeared in Kureishi's *Borderlines* at the Royal Court in the early 1980s and taken the central female role in *Majdhar* playing a young Pakistani woman whose husband leaves her after an arranged marriage. Wolf's role as Tania was strongly criticised in a film that was deemed to have treated Asian women as stereotypes. In addition, as Wolf herself acknowledged, Tania's act of baring her breasts became the defining moment of the role with a lasting effect on critics.[35] Nevertheless, it would be wrong to see Wolf's performance as bound by the more voyeuristic elements of that scene or indeed the cliché of the Asian girl trying to avoid an arranged marriage. Tania is, as we have seen, a character on the outside of the story, and the role is affected by some of the incoherences of the plot; her switch from Omar to Johnny as a possible escape route is underwritten. Nevertheless, like Warnecke and unlike Day-Lewis, Wolf does create a character who changes as the film progresses and emerges as a stronger woman than the spoilt girl of the earlier scenes. The first shot of Tania shows her as the middle daughter, looking up from under her forehead between her two sisters, but she emerges as a young woman who wants not only to escape from her family but to have knowledge – of business, of relationships, of the world – and it is this which she gradually gains. This is shown in the way in which Wolf plays Tania as gaining in confidence as the film develops, her movements becoming more assured as she walks alone into the launderette at the opening or down the stairs, with a little smile at her own glamour, into her father's party. Tania's confrontations with her father and Rachel reveal frustration and anger but it is Wolf's ability to show how Tania absorbs what is happening which gives her character weight. This is backed up by camerawork which, albeit briefly, puts her in the centre of the frame. In an early scene on the veranda with Omar, she is filmed mainly in long-shot or from behind. Only at the end of the scene do we see her full face as she makes her comment about families. As the film progresses, though, a series of close-ups reveal her seriousness: Tania's face is shown, eager for new excitement, as she joins the male group in front of Johnny; she challenges Rachel at the opening but absorbs what she says; she watches, isolated, as Omar and Johnny leave her after Nasser's party. Her final scene with Johnny is not a plea for help but a warning based on what she has learnt about the family business, her father's decline and Omar's character; Johnny has a different kind of knowledge but Wolf's self-possession and reflectiveness, particularly in the close-ups in this scene, mean that Tania's position is not undermined. In its elusive opening up of possibilities, perhaps Tania's disappearance from the railway platform can be compared with that of Julie Christie's Liz in *Billy Liar* (1963). But Wolf, appropriately for the 1980s, has made Tania's frustrations into a more serious, more political statement about a young woman's desire for knowledge as well as freedom.

Like Warnecke, Wolf subsequently found herself restricted by attitudes to black actors but she appears to have carved out a substantial career, particularly in the theatre, committing herself to innovative and unusual work there. Shortly after the success of *Laundrette*, she wrote about the stereotyping of black actors, with women's roles still confined to 'prostitutes, athletes and handmaidens'.[36] She has had television roles including two soaps, *Albion Market*, and more significantly *Coronation Street* in 1990/1. She was quoted as liking the latter because it 'belonged to the here and now of Britain'; it 'has never forced racial issues' and race and religion 'have never been mentioned in storylines' involving her character.[37] The other major British soap, *EastEnders*, came in for criticism, though, and Wolf apparently turned down the offer of a part 'when the producers failed to respond to her sharp questioning about WHAT ELSE the character did, apart from run the corner shop'.[38] She left *Coronation Street* to direct a new play and to co-found the Kali Theatre company, but in the 1990s settled in the USA, where she has appeared in controversial new plays such as Tony Kushner's *Homebody/Kabul*, which opened in New York in 2001, and interesting revivals such as a new version of Lorca's *The House of Bernarda Alba* in Los Angeles in 2002. Her film work has, by contrast, been very limited, which may be the reason why the *Companion to Contemporary Black British Culture*, published seventeen years after *Laundrette* was released, described Tania as Wolf's 'most memorable role to date'.[39]

If Day-Lewis, Warnecke and Wolf were the newcomers, Field, Jaffrey and Seth were, in their own ways, the experienced old hands for whom *Laundrette* represented a rather different opportunity. It was a film in which they could build on existing reputations and perhaps transform them into something more. Field's was a particularly poignant case. Her first screen breakthroughs came when she was twenty-one years old in two of the key films of the British 'new wave', *The Entertainer* (1960) and *Saturday Night and Sunday Morning*. In such films, she worked in a realist tradition and held her own in movies dominated by male stars. After that, though, her career seems to have become a series of comebacks. Her appearance in *Alfie* (1966) was heralded as a 'return',[40] since marriage and an unsuccessful attempt at Hollywood had taken her out of the public eye. In 1980 she was described as making another comeback, this time on television with *Shoestring* and *Buccaneer* – 'Taking off again Shirley Anne', as the *Daily Mail* put it, welcoming her return after 'the lean years'.[41] But Field was still seen more consistently on television panel shows, and the release of *My Beautiful Laundrette* was presented as another 'Field's Renaissance', with Frears quoted as saying that 'it is iniquitous, a tragedy, that she hasn't been used more'.[42] Consistent references were also made to her earlier career as an actress and a glamorous movie star, when she 'acted with Olivier and Robert Wagner, and was romanced by Frank Sinatra'.[43] It was a pattern that made Field feel rather 'peeved' about being 'rediscovered every decade. "I'm fed up with being the critics' darling every ten years."'[44]

In an evocative comment in publicity interviews for *Laundrette*, Field remarks that 'it is exciting for me to be playing the women of the girls I used to play'.[45] She brings to the part a regretful air which indeed equates to the loss of girlhood and a slight uncertainty about what maturity has brought. The pattern of the narrative moves her character from a central position to a marginal one and so Field's performance involves a controlled letting-go of precarious happiness. Field plays down both the emotional insecurities of the character and the rather tarty aura that seems to be a feature of the script. The key elements of her performance are her husky voice and her direct gaze. The wide-eyed, undeviating look which focuses with absolute attention on the individual she is dealing with is used to give the impression of loving absorption and concern. Thus, at the beginning of the film, Field continues to look directly and lovingly at Omar, even when, as at the bar, Nasser is talking or when, as in the garage, she herself is talking to Nasser about Omar. At the launderette opening, this direct look is aimed at Nasser as she tells him, 'You are sometimes [pause] careless', but the words and look are then softened by a gesture of the hands as she asks him to dance. Similarly, when Tania is deliberately rude and hurtful, Field's face shows little emotion but she refuses to turn her gaze away from her; when she finally responds verbally, her look is quizzical and sympathetic rather than angry. The effect of such looks is to define Rachel not only as frank but as someone whose own thoughts and motivations take second place to those of the people she loves.

Field's other resource for the character is her voice. Her accent is refined, as if Rachel had learnt to speak differently from Johnny (whose mother she knows), and she speaks softly and with relatively little variation in tone. But the nuances are considerable. Sometimes, as in the first sex scene, her voice has a breathy warmth which belies the rather anxious, nagging words scripted for Rachel. Sometimes her voice allows the anxiety to be expressed but almost regretfully, as when she tells Tania, 'Nothing has ever waited for me except [and she briefly shifts her gaze] your father.' In her final scene, when Field's facial expressions are some-what withheld from us by the camera position, shadows across her face and the lines of the grille, her voice carries the controlled emotion. It is higher and lighter when she tells Nasser of her decision that they should part, rises again when she says 'love', breaks slightly over 'money' and resumes control when she says 'you'. It drops and darkens when she refers to his wife as 'a brilliant woman' and, in a reiteration of her first scene, reveals part of her body, this time covered with a rash. Looking frankly at him, she delivers her final words softly, with restraint and control, as she defines their past for Nasser; 'we've had a time, [pause] a nice time'. With this performance, *My Beautiful Laundrette* connects not only with the 'new wave' films of Shirley Anne Field's 'girls' but also with those acting traditions of British cinema in which restraint is precisely a means of expressing strong emotion.[46]

My Beautiful Laundrette did not perhaps effect the breakthrough Field may have wished for but it seems to have given new impetus to her career. In 1989 she recalled that the American success of the film had taken her to Hollywood and into the soap *Santa Barbara*.[47] She had parts in two films in the USA but returned to Britain to feature in an adaptation of an early Martin Amis novel, *The Rachel Papers* (1989), and another film for Channel 4, *Hear My Song* (1991). She also returned to British television drama and more recently has had roles in some of the staples of British television, including *The Bill* (2000), *Dalziel and Pascoe* (1999) and *Where the Heart is* (2001). Following the pattern of her career, it could count as a modest but welcome renaissance.

My Beautiful Laundrette was also an important landmark for Roshan Seth and Saeed Jaffrey, though not as a comeback. Both were experienced actors who were best known for their roles in the Raj television series and films. Seth had taken major parts with the National Theatre and the RSC, played Nehru in *Gandhi* (1982) as well as roles in *Passage to India* and *Indiana Jones and the Temple of Doom* (1984). Jaffrey had worked in theatre and film in India, the USA and Britain and had appeared in one of Kureishi's earlier plays at the Royal Court. He too had appeared in *Gandhi* and *Passage to India* as well as in *The Far Pavilions* (1984) and *Jewel in the Crown*. Kureishi maintained that he had wanted to rescue Jaffrey and Seth from 'bit parts in Easterns'[48] and both reward him with fine performances.

Jaffrey's performance is perhaps easy to underestimate given his ebullient image. In fact, it is a performance that handles the satirical thrust of the character with subtlety. Jaffrey expresses Nasser's warmth as well as his self-satisfaction. He plays the smooth operator who at various moments has to calm others such as Salim down. Jaffrey's walk, with his hands in his pockets, is confident, his voice smooths the Pakistani inflections[49] and he uses a broad smile, raised eyebrows and expansive gestures at moments of relaxation with his cronies. He is much shorter than most of the actors he is playing with but retains control by avoiding looking up at them, using a sideways and upwards movement of his eyes rather than craning his neck when he is addressing them. He uses gestures confidently to express the character as well as to underline the words; thus, the flourish with which he gives Omar a bucket to start his new job indicates the infinite possibilities Nasser believes he is opening up for his nephew, while a turn of the hand which accompanies the question to Johnny – 'Can you keep this zoo under control?' – is made more steely by the stiff arm and the way in which the movement of the hand finishes with a point downward with the index finger. His confident, warm manner is reinforced by the use of brown and orange colour to dress and light him, particularly in scenes in the office.

In the first part of the film, Jaffrey varies this approach in two ways. Sometimes he underplays the lines, making his voice softer and his face less mobile; he does this, for instance, when he shares his philosophy with Omar in the bar or when, languorous on his bed, his voice hardens when he asks Omar about the launderette – 'What are you doing, boy?' This has the effect of allowing us to see the businessman behind the front and of downplaying some of the script's more rhetorical turns of phrase in line with the realist approach of much of the film. At other points, Jaffrey over-animates his gestures and facial expressions, as when he erupts with rage when a boy throws food into a drying machine or when he shouts at the poet whom he gets Johnny to evict.

Both of these performance variations are used in the later scenes of the film to indicate Nasser's declining grip on events. The rages become his characteristic approach to members of his family. An off-screen screech, for instance, heralds Nasser's approach to the veranda where his wife is casting spells, and Jaffrey uses flailing arm gestures, initially to attack her and then to defend himself against her response. During the launderette opening, Jaffrey's animated facial expressions and sharp tone indicate increased exasperation with Tania, and his final conversations with her are shouting matches. But the less animated mode is a feature of his final moments at the bar with Rachel, when he turns his still face away as she leaves, and he adopts a quiet, nostalgic tone for the meeting with Papa, once again downplaying the rhetoric of his criticism of Pakistan. In some senses, Jaffrey's performance moves from the broadly satirical to the ironic mode more strongly associated with that of Seth as Papa. The final shot of him, though, the facial muscles deflated as he takes in the fact of Tania's disappearance, is of a man who is truly lost.

Seth's angular, pale cheekbones and aquiline nose are very different from Jaffrey's flat, round, brown face and the contrast in appearance and manners between the two brothers is reflected in the performances. Papa is generally filmed in harsh white or blue light and his *mise-en-scène* has none of the sensuality associated with Nasser. Seth uses gesture in a more limited way and does not so much engage with the other actors as talk at them; in scenes with Omar, he often looks down or talks to his back. His face remains unexpressive when he makes his barbed comments or, as in the first scene, when he jokes with Omar about his unused penis. Seth's voice can be harsh when he uses the crude language Papa is given – 'my tool would drop off', 'bloody arse', 'bum liability' – but even during his invective against Omar's clumsy toenail cutting, Seth's raised voice does not dominate since it has to compete with Omar's conversation with Johnny and the noise of passing trains. Generally, the voice is controlled and relatively quiet, giving the impression of a man who relishes language but is disassociated from his feelings.

In an interview when the film was released, Day-Lewis suggested that Papa is the most important character in the film and one who affected

8. *Papa and Johnny about to begin their battle for Omar.* (*Source*: BFI
Collections, courtesy of FilmFour)

Johnny's actions: 'it is through the father that we see the re-emergence
of Johnny's conscience and the beginnings of social awareness. He
comes under the influence of this very charismatic man and so will-
ingly gives himself to the dictatorship of Omar and fulfills Omar's wish
to punish him.'[50] This strikes me as an interesting example of an actor
creating a rationale for his character which is actually not borne out
in the film, either in the narrative or Seth's performance. Despite his
hunched shoulders and lesser stature, Seth holds his own with Day-
Lewis, but he offers a portrayal of a charismatic man who has lost his
powers, as the key scene between Papa and Johnny in the launderette
shows. Seth smiles as he softly but precisely expresses contempt for the
decor, articulating the Ps in 'Pinner' and 'pink rinse' while the tone of
the voice lifts to a higher register to express his disdain for 'underpant
cleaner[s]'. His voice and movements are restrained as he sits to deliver
the question 'Or are you still a fascist?' He turns his back on Johnny as
if to control himself and, although he turns to face the camera again,
his next words – 'Help me' – are delivered softly, against the noise
of the spin dryers. Like Jaffrey, Seth underplays Kureishi's rhetorical
flourishes, and the speech on the need for education which follows is
delivered with quiet compassion as the large, liquid eyes directly fix on
Johnny. Seth's voice is firm and unexpressive but the demotic 'Right?'

at the end of the speech has a tentative quality, as if Papa realises the humiliation inherent in pleading with Johnny. His final words – 'not a bad dump' – are spoken fastidiously, as if he is amused by his own ingratiating adoption of slang. Throughout the scene, the tone of voice is ironic, bringing to Papa's own pleas the amused contempt with which he treats the launderette.

Of the two actors, Jaffrey was probably the one more affected by *Laundrette*'s success. Seth continued his connection with Kureishi, appearing in *London Kills Me* (1991) and *The Buddha of Suburbia* (1993) on television. He has enjoyed an international career, playing cameo roles of various ethnicities as well as appearing in Mira Nair's *Mississippi Masala* (1991) and *Monsoon Wedding* (2002). Jaffrey, however, has made himself a formidable presence on the British screen, finally being awarded an OBE in 1995 for services to drama and turning up at the palace to collect it in a 1942 Rolls-Royce. Given Jaffrey's long experience, it would clearly be wrong to suggest that *My Beautiful Laundrette* launched his career but it certainly helped him to reposition himself as an actor. Shortly after the film's British release, he was quoted as saying that '*Laundrette* gave me the chance to show off my own ability' and the *Daily Mail* agreed that, after a long career, 'with *My Beautiful Laundrette* ... he reached celebrity status', noting the irony 'that he finally found fame with the lowest budget film of his career'.[51] *Laundrette* persists as a critical turning point in later accounts of his success. Thus, *Eastern Eye* in 1996 reported him still saying 'I was lucky to work on that film' and concurred that 'the star of hit films like *The Man Who Would be King* and *Gandhi* really made it big in Britain when he landed the role of Nasser in *My Beautiful Laundrette*'.[52] Yet another career review, in 1998, recounted that 'Jaffrey's good times started with a bang in August 1985', linking the success of *Laundrette* at Edinburgh with his appearance in Ry Kapoor's last film, *Ram Teri Gamg Maili*, which ran for a year in India.[53] Jaffrey's extraordinarily varied career is applauded for expanding the boundaries of what Asian actors could achieve. If, as *Eastern Eye* claimed, 'no Asian project is complete – be it in Britain and India – on stage, television, radio or cinema' without his presence, he is also praised for opening up possibilities for others; Meera Syal, herself a successful actress, author and scriptwriter, is quoted as saying that 'he is responsible for the turn around in Asian drama since the Eighties'.[54]

THREE
Continuations: *Laundrette's* Reputation

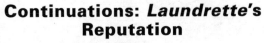

In Chapter 1, we traced the beginnings of *My Beautiful Laundrette*, a process of becoming which involved exhibition, publicity and reviewing, practices of political and cultural recognition as well as those of production. But films are not defined for ever by their first reception; some that find an initial audience disappear while the reputation of others is established well after the initial run. *My Beautiful Laundrette* is still available on video and DVD, still screened on television and shown in film societies and festivals.[1] It has never lost its reputation as an interesting and successful film, but that reputation has different meanings in different situations. In this chapter, I want to look at how *Laundrette* fared in the nineties and to examine some of the various cultural and educational contexts in which it is still promoted as a film worth seeing and indeed writing about. This is an ongoing reception process, in which the film, now reproduced on video and DVD, is continually recommended, used and passed on to others and its defining characteristics reinforced, reinterpreted or refused. It can be usefully thought about in terms of the lists to which the film is added. *My Beautiful Laundrette* is perhaps unusual in having such a wide range of different statuses and its success lies in the way in which it continues to function, as we shall see, as a breakthrough British Asian movie, an exemplary academic text, a British ambassador, a Valentine's Day offering or simply a favourite film. More generally, looking at how *My Beautiful Laundrette* works in this way provides a model of this process for other successful films.

CULTURAL IDENTITY AND BLACK FILM-MAKING

As we saw in Chapter 1, the ICA conference drew on the experience of black film-makers and cultural theorists in developing new agendas and

9. *Advert for the video of* My Beautiful Laundrette, *undated*, TV Times. (*Source*: Flashback)

building on the opportunities offered in particular by Channel 4. While there were difficulties and differences, there was a strong sense of the potential for black film-making in a changing and exciting theoretical framework. Four years later, in 1992, a British Film Institute conference discussed the prospects for black intervention in television and gave a number of the ICA participants an opportunity to reflect on what had happened. Stuart Hall continued to draw attention to 'the vigour, vitality and diversity of the black cultural revolution which has exploded across the British scene'[2] and again resisted the essentialism of the 'segment-market conception of the audience – black programmes for black audiences, white programmes for white audiences', suggesting that 'it is precisely the overlaps, the flow-between and crossovers which have underpinned what advances have so far been made' (p. 19). He recognised that 'without the primary funding and visual showcasing of television, there would have been no British "film renaissance" (shortlived as it was)' (p. 24) and suggested that the black independent sector needed to reassess its strategies faced with a new emphasis in television on marketing and competition. Paul Gilroy was sharper and more critical, suggesting that black practitioners were abandoning broader aspirations in the pursuit of the limited money on offer: 'the political and economic divisions of the bleak present became impossible to avoid when the desire for racial justice and compensation for cultural marginality was replaced by the need to find serious strategies and credible tactics capable of advancing the position of black film makers'.[3]

Commentators reviewing black film-making at the end of the nineties felt that Gilroy's pessimism was justified. Karen Alexander summed up 'the failure of any sustained development of the past decade' and suggested that the hybrid nature of British culture was specifically problematic for British cinema; 'it seems ironic that the complexities of black British culture can be encapsulated in a love song or a dance track but fail to find articulation in one of the most modern art forms, cinema'.[4] Jim Pines, also reviewing the decade, concurred, believing that 'the emergence of a completely new cultural and political agenda in Britain ... has temporarily halted any radically new interventions in the area of black representation'.[5] Sarita Malik suggested that black film-makers have gone backwards, being 'still considered as "minority artists"' and 'forced to subsidize their own work or move beyond Britain's shores, just as the Black-British filmmakers of the 1960s and 1970s were inclined to do'.[6]

For many of those involved in the precarious activity of making British films, *My Beautiful Laundrette* has been an inspiration and a measure of success. Isaac Julien, a young film-maker whose work with Sankofa had been discussed at the ICA, recalls that 'I could relate to *My Beautiful Laundrette* even though I found the identities of Omar and Johnny very problematic ... When we were shooting *Passion [of Remembrance]* we were going to cut the kissing scene but, after seeing *Laundrette*, I insisted on keeping it in.'[7] Julien's diary of the making of *Young Soul Rebels* (1991) records a wary rivalry with Kureishi, then working on *London Kills Me*, but *Laundrette*'s continuing function as a cross-over model is clear, even though Colin McCabe tried to dampen it down; he argued with Julien and producer Nadine Marsh-Edwards that 'even if the film were as successful as *My Beautiful Laundrette*, with a packed-out West End run, followed by a circuit release, it still wouldn't reach a young black audience'.[8]

My Beautiful Laundrette's example was of especial importance to British-Asian film-makers. In 1996, Malik suggested that they were in a particularly difficult position, 'culturally marginalised (both critically and institutionally) within an already culturally marginalised Black British film sector'.[9] In fact, as the 1990s came to a close, the commercial and critical successes were associated with British-Asian film-making, and writers and directors looked back to *My Beautiful Laundrette* as the first step that made it possible. As the thread is extended, the list links *My Beautiful Laundrette* to *Bhaji on the Beach* (1993) to *East is East* (1999) to *Bend It Like Beckham* (2002). All are films that deal with the hybridity and mixing of black British nationality; all take such diversity for granted, the mainsprings of the plot lying elsewhere; and all attempt a cross-over, often in the face of industry resistance, so as not to confine the films to either black or art house audiences. As Khan Din, the writer of *East is East*, put it, 'Each film that comes along pushes the boundary of film forward. *My Beautiful Laundrette*, then *Bhaji on the Beach*. *East is East* has carried it a bit further.'[10]

East is East offers a particularly interesting example of how the success of *My Beautiful Laundrette* could be built on. The film was strongly associated with its writer, who carried much of the publicity at its opening in November 1999. Khan Din had a bit part in *Laundrette* and played the lead in *Sammy and Rosie* but more importantly, like Kureishi, he had made a reputation as a playwright at the Royal Court Theatre; indeed, the film was an adaptation of his original play with a number of actors from that cast. Khan Din approached Frears to direct, before getting Damien O'Donnell to do so; he wanted a non-Asian director, it was reported, 'because he was insistent that the film should find a cross-over audience'.[11] The BBC supported the development costs but was made nervous by the failure of the Kureishi-scripted *My Son the Fanatic* (1997), which suffered from poor distribution. *East is East* was funded by FilmFour at a cost of £2 million. Khan Din, like Kureishi, regarded himself as having no PR responsibility for the Asian communities ('I don't write to please any particular part of the community – I write to please myself'[12]) and drew on British sources for the strong elements of Northern humour and seaside farce in the film. The portrayal of the harsh father (brilliantly played by Om Puri who injects moments of doubt and humanity into the part) and, in particular, the stereotyping of virtually all the young women drew complaints. But, like *Laundrette*, *East is East* presented a bleak situation but was praised by critics for being warm and funny. Khan Din refused to define his script as Asian, an approach commended by Kureishi, who commented approvingly that 'over the years we're going to become so integrated into British life that an Asian movie will be no different to say *The Full Monty*'.[13]

Kureishi's comparison with the phenomenally successful British film of 1997 indicates the difference, however, between *My Beautiful Laundrette* and *East is East* in terms of marketing and distribution. Producer Leslee Udwin reportedly fought film distributors who, she said, told her: 'It will not cross. It's a ghettoised film' and, in the end, £1 million went on prints and advertising with the emphasis on selling it to youthful audiences as 'a funny and accessible comedy'.[14] Two hundred prints allowed for a blanket release and the film was reported to have recouped its production costs in a fortnight.[15] Miramax bought the US rights early and the connection back to *Laundrette* was also recognised there: 'with its rich mix of social criticism, domestic comedy and kitchen-sink melodrama, *East is East* confirms a strain of contemporary British cinema that first came to international acclaim with 1985's *My Beautiful Laundrette*'.[16] The film took £10.3 million pounds in Britain, $4.1 million in the USA, and was widely seen in Europe. Looking back on this commercial success, Parminder Vir remarked that 'the only other film that came close to that was *My Beautiful Laundrette*'.[17] But *East is East* was certainly operating with a very different selling regime. The film's release was accompanied by newspaper features about how 'it's very trendy now to be Indian'[18] and a celebratory attitude to its mixed-race cast. By the time of *Bend It Like Beckham*, this became a flood. The director Gurinder Chadha 'traces her interest in film-making back to seeing *My Beautiful Laundrette*'[19] and her first film, *Bhaji on the Beach*, had been, like *Laundrette*, an unexpected success. But the release of *Bend It Like Beckham* was that of a mainstream hit. It went out on 450 prints in April 2002 alongside a massive publicity campaign and took £2 million pounds on its opening weekend. Like *Laundrette*, it was a festival success, picking up the prize for Best European Film at the 2002 Sydney Film Festival, for instance, but it was also a commercial success in India and, more remarkably, the USA. Chadha was at pains to present it as a film with 'universal' rather than 'Asian-specific' appeal, stressing that 'British audiences identify characters regardless of their background'.[20] For some, the themes of identity and hybridity that linked *My Beautiful Laundrette* to *Bend It Like Beckham* were pulled rather thin; Claire Monk criticised it for covering old ground, suggesting that its 'preoccupation with finding novel ways to shake up old stereotypes and notions of British identity ... has become a staple of recent British films'.[21] And indeed the unashamedly commercial approach of such a film is a far cry from the discussions and predictions at the ICA in 1988. Nevertheless, the success of *East is East* and *Bend It Like Beckham* in pummelling the commercial sector into putting their stories on the screen is significant. Chadha, who had gone to the USA because she felt the potential signalled by the success of *Bhaji* could not be realised in Britain in the mid-nineties, felt in 2002 that 'there are greater opportunities to create innovative, widely appealing black and Asian films in the UK than there are in the US'.[22] This would fit Parminder Vir's analysis of the link between the success of Bollywood films with British audiences, the potential market in India for British films and the commercial success of British Asian and Indian diaspora films; 'there are now more possibilities than ever before', she argued, 'for developing a uniquely British Asian film industry'.[23]

Vir's emphasis on audiences reminds us that one of the things these films did was to create and sustain audiences that responded to such work. The appeal was to the young – *Asian Age* reported that *East is East*'s success was with second- and third-generation Asians while 'their parents sit at home with their heads in their hands'.[24] Sukhdev Sandhu argued that *My Beautiful Laundrette* and Kureishi's work more generally had helped to create such audiences. He describes the experience of watching the film, as a teenager, with his reluctant parents, who had arrived in England from India in the 1960s:

> All I had seen were the tantalising trailers: the film looked youthful; it was about people like me. The night it was on TV, I swept the carpet, prepared snacks – some Nice biscuits and a cup of hot milk each – and sat my parents down. On the walls of the sitting room was the obligatory picture of the Sikh holy shrine, the Golden Temple in Amritsar ... Everything was perfect except, it turned out, the film itself.[25]

Sandhu recalls that by the time the film got to Nasser and Rachel 'humping away ... I was having doubts', and when Tania showed her breasts 'my father flipped. "Why are you showing us such filth? Is this what you do at school? Is this the kind of thing you listen to on the radio?" he yelled before lunging at me' (p. 34). Despite or because of this, Sandhu credits Kureishi with offering 'for the first time a recognisable portrait of British Asian life', crediting him with 'a pivotal role in helping second- and third-generation Asians think of themselves – and be thought of – as young people' (p. 34) who could participate in creating and enjoying a new culture; 'he changed the lives of many young Asians. He also inspired them to become artists' (p. 35). Sandhu points to the explosion of interest in things Asian, citing *East is East*, but stretching the list further to include the highly successful all-Asian television comedy series *Goodness Gracious Me*. 'The work of these artists', he concludes, 'is saturated with optimism' (p. 35), the optimism that *My Beautiful Laundrette*, for all its seedy settings and controversial characters, so vividly expressed.

GAY ROMANCES

If *My Beautiful Laundrette* continued to be a reference point and inspiration for black and Asian film-makers and critics, it had far less impact on gay film-making and theoretical writing. As we have seen, the film was welcomed on its release at least in part for the fresh and unforced handling of gay sexuality. But while its representation of a gay love affair was an important factor in the claims made about the film's hybridity, specifically gay responses to the film become harder to find as we move away from the initial reaction. In this discursive context, looking for *My Beautiful Laundrette* is also a question of registering footnotes and absences.

Thus, we note the absence of gay and lesbian culture in recent academic literature on British cinema. Robert Murphy's two collections, for instance, find room for essays on black British cinema but gay representations are dealt with more obliquely through essays on 'new romanticism' and 'sexual plurality', and a similar absence may be noted in another collection, *British Cinema Past and Present*.[26] *Laundrette* does not feature in the influential work of Richard Dyer, though he does refer to it as one of 'a crop of sharp, engaging lesbian and gay films and tele-series produced rather surprisingly in Britain in the late 80s and 90s'.[27] Although British films did feature in the development of queer theory in the 1990s, it is *Looking for Langston* (1988), *Young Soul Rebels* (1991) and particularly *Edward II* (1991) which feature in the lists associated with queer cinema; note, for instance, the use of *Looking for Langston* in *How Do I Look? Queer Film and Video*, the inclusion of *Edward II* in Paul Burston's list in 'End of the Road', and the essay on Jarman in *Out Takes. Essays on Queer Theory*.[28]

There are various complex reasons for *Laundrette*'s absences in this context. There was initially the question of authorship. Frears was not a gay film-maker and so lacked the auteur position that could be identified for Jarman and Julien. In the context of black and Asian film-making, *My Beautiful Laundrette* was Kureishi's film and, despite his refusal to take on PR functions for that constituency, he was eager, as we have seen, to position himself and the film within debates about black representation. This writer-as-auteur position did not work for Kureishi in relation to gay film culture, particularly when the second film he scripted, while retaining the inter-racial hybridity, featured extensive heterosexual coupling. In addition, *My Beautiful Laundrette* did not refer even obliquely to Aids, which, in the mid-eighties, was becoming a dominant and troubling concern for gay film-makers and their audiences. The film therefore did not fit the context of gay authorship and was seen as something of a one-off rather than the beginning of a recognised body of exemplary work. Derek Jarman, whose *Caravaggio* was successfully released in 1986, a year after *Laundrette*, provided a much more usable model.

In some ways, it is more surprising that *My Beautiful Laundrette* was not picked up in the development of queer theory. Indeed, one reference book, *Images in the Dark*, categorises the film as 'an early and definitive example of New Queer Cinema', and the film's emphasis on hybridity, incoherence and performance may have fitted the tendency of 'queer reception' to 'stand outside clearcut and essentialising categories of sexual identity'.[29] Indeed, B. Ruby Rich, looking at queer films dealing with cross-race dynamics, suggests in a footnote that '*My Beautiful Laundrette* constituted a precedent for much of the work that followed on both sides of the Atlantic', but does not discuss it in her article because of 'my emphasis on lower-budget, non-theatrical film and video'.[30] Ironically, *Young Soul Rebels* is included despite a budget, admittedly five years later, double that of *Laundrette* and a (less successful) theatrical release.

But two factors militated against *My Beautiful Laundrette* emerging as an exemplary queer film. First, when avant-garde aesthetics were the issue (rather than black representation), *Laundrette* hardly counted as an independent film, being seen, as Rich indicates, as a mainstream Channel 4 production. *Laundrette*'s cross-over success worked against it here, so that one comparison concluded: 'Julien goes further than Kureishi's fundamentally populist, realist framework.'[31] Second, as Andy Medhurst puts it, 'queer audiences have rapidly learned the survival skills

of refashioning heterosexual images to suit our own purposes',[32] and
queer theory's emphasis on camp, on outing the hidden and asserting
the possibilities of different readings of mainstream films, did not fit
particularly well with *My Beautiful Laundrette*'s upfront sexuality and
political edge. Thus, in this context, European and US classics like *The
Cabinet of Dr Caligari* (1920), *The Wizard of Oz* (1939) and *Gentlemen
Prefer Blondes* (1953) were more useful to queer theory, more likely
to 'yield a wider range of non-straight readings because sexual things
could not be stated baldly'.[33] If queer theory is, as Dyer has suggested,
'specially interested in manifestations of male–male sexual attraction
where you wouldn't expect to find it, where it's been diverted or
repressed or else obliquely expressed or unknowingly sublimated',[34]
then *My Beautiful Laundrette* clearly does not fit the bill; indeed, the
relationship between Omar and Johnny, particularly the sex scene at
the launderette opening, fits much more readily into an earlier concern
with positive images which queer theory was at least questioning and
in some cases rejecting.

But *Laundrette*'s ongoing reputation in other areas of gay film culture
indicates that there is still a demand for such pleasures. 'We were bored
with tired seventies notions of positive role models,' wrote one group
of editors,[35] but while the 'representation of gay men' approach might
be deemed theoretically unsophisticated in the 1990s, it still seems to
have an appeal. For *Laundrette* still retains an important place in gay
film lists, where it is described as offering the positive pleasures of a
gay romance. As one US guide puts it, 'for gay audiences, it's the
sizzling (and matter-of-factly treated) sexual chemistry between Omar
and Johnny that caps a contemporary classic', while another British
guide wryly emphasises the film's utopian aspects, starting its sum-
mary with 'Racism falls victim to the hormone fairy' and ending with
a vignette of the film as 'a small rainbow arching over a confused and
grimy cityscape'.[36] In such guides, gay authorship is less of an issue;
an Australian index starts its entry for the film with the suggestion that
'from one of the best straight directors to deal with gay and lesbian
issues comes this gem', while *Images in the Dark* includes Kureishi in
its list of writers and comments that 'the two characters' gayness is
open and matter-of-fact, loving and sexual and, most importantly, not
troubling to themselves'.[37]

Websites have, of course, extended the possibilities of this kind of
listing. A Canadian website included *Laundrette* alongside *Gone with
the Wind* (1939) and *Breakfast at Tiffany's* (1961) as a 'romantic title'

10. *Johnny and Omar at the heart of the gay romance. See Chapter 2 for a discussion of the way in which the space between the characters is used.* (*Source*: BFI Collections, courtesy of FilmFour)

for Valentine's Day, claiming that the list proved that 'movie makers have come up with plenty of classics when it comes to tugging at heartstrings'.[38] Web retailers also try to get the film into their gay canons: BlackStar linked *My Beautiful Laundrette* as a possible purchase for those buying other British work such as *Maurice* (1987), *Beautiful Thing* (1996)[39] and the television series *Queer as Folk* (1999/2000), while Amazon quoted a customer review from Portland, Oregon, which enthused:

> You say you want a 'can't fail' way to get into that new man's heart/ pants? Invite him over for dinner and a double-bill of *My Beautiful Laundrette* and *Maurice*. If he doesn't dissolve into a mushy romantic mess from these two, check his pulse ... Sure, you'll want to be the sweat between the protagonists. But I wanted to live in the world this film created just to meet and spend more time with the fascinating characters.[40]

PopcornQ Movies directly quotes from the *Ultimate Guide*'s review of the film, demonstrating how this list activity feeds off itself, while less commercial contexts are offered by individual websites which continue to add *My Beautiful Laundrette* to their authors' personal lists. 'Chuck Griffith', for instance, provides his list of Best Gay Themed Films, suggesting that *My Beautiful Laundrette* 'is better than most gay films', though he adds, 'I would say that there isn't much to choose from, sadly'.[41]

ACADEMIC ACCEPTANCE

In academic writing, films are chosen on the grounds of pleasure more often than authors might admit, but they also have to function in an argument, work to make a point in a more abstract discussion. One of the reasons for *My Beautiful Laundrette*'s continuing presence is the way it has been picked up in the rapidly expanding literature on British cinema. In British work, this can be divided somewhat schematically into two groups which often overlap – those discussing *Laundrette* as the perfect Channel 4 film and those using it to demonstrate theories of hybridity and cultural identity. In both cases, this 1990s work situates *My Beautiful Laundrette* in the Thatcherite eighties and uses the film, and particularly Kureishi's account of it, to explain the contested area of nationality and culture in that period.

In the 1990s, as British television increasingly faced commercial pressures and fragmentation, accounts of the creation and development of Channel 4 were a way of examining the impact of change. It was important, also, to review what Channel 4 had done in terms of British cinema's precarious claims to independence. John Hill and Christopher Williams give largely favourable accounts which acknowledge how, at a crucial and desperate time for British cinema, Channel 4 opened up new production and distribution possibilities and created a distinctive type of film. *My Beautiful Laundrette* is deemed significant and exemplary in these accounts. Thus, Williams includes it, with *The Draughtsman's Contract* and *Chariots of Fire*, as one of 'the three defining British films of the last decade'[42] and argues that Film on Four provided a space for the British art film to emerge, bringing to British cinema some of the characteristics of its European counterpart: 'individual identity, sexuality, psychological complexity, anomie, episodicness, interiority, ambiguity, style' (p. 198). Williams suggests that this is most evident in *My Beautiful Laundrette*,

> in which central questions of sexual identity are mixed with discussion of race, economics and generation difference and where the action constantly swings back and forth between the social and the individual in a manner which may not always work ... and in which the ideas may be rigged to some extent but which compels admiration for its vigour and attempt at comprehensiveness. (p. 199)

John Caughie also argues that Film on Four changed what was meant by a 'made for television' film and developed 'an art cinema which was almost incidentally shown on television'.[43] He goes on to suggest that *My Beautiful Laundrette* not only illustrates what Film on Four made possible in the 1980s but also what might not be possible later. He analyses the film by posing the question as to whether 'such a film could be made in such a way in the late 90s' and suggests that the lack of stars and an established scriptwriter, the narrative untidiness, the excessive number of social themes, the 'mosaic of issues and situations' (p. 198) would all have

> made it 'too hard to sell' in the 1990s. The unexpected success of *My Beautiful Laundrette* in the international market of the 1980s seems to have been replaced by an expectation of success in the 1990s ... [and] a shift in dominance in the creative process away from the untidiness of writers and directors towards the more surgical skills of producers and script writers. (p. 199)

Thus for Williams the film helped to define a genre while for Caughie *My Beautiful Laundrette*, even in the process of defining Film on Four's version of art cinema, provided a still more important example of a film that evaded the limiting demands that were to be placed on the genre. The fleeting, utopian moments offered in the film's narrative are here paralleled by an institutional account in which the genesis of the film itself is possible only in a romantic and brief moment.

In institutional terms, then, *My Beautiful Laundrette* is one of a number of films that helped to define a Channel 4 film as something new in British cinema. For both Williams and Caughie, this is due to the vigorous and sometimes untidy way in which it addresses issues of individual identity and social formations. These themes are taken up more fully by the critics who approach the film most centrally through an account of cultural difference. Such critics, of whom Hill is the most influential, link *My Beautiful Laundrette* with *Sammy and Rosie Get Laid* and use both to consider, as Hill puts it, 'the ways in which they challenge traditional conceptions of "race" and celebrate the emergence of new kinds of hybrid identities'[44] in the context of the right-wing economic and social politics of Thatcher's post-Falkland government. Hill's detailed account starts with a quotation from Kureishi, whose commentaries on his own work are used extensively, and is interlaced with quotations from cultural theorists such as Hall, Gilroy, Mercer and Bhabha. Hill links the films to the ideas about 'the constructedness and fluidity of social identities' (p. 207) promoted in postmodern thinking and suggests that 'such formulations are helpful in accounting for the strong sense of the criss-crossed nature of identities' (p. 208) in the Kureishi/Frears films. Hill's headings – 'Living with difference' and '"In-betweenness"' – indicate his emphasis on Hall's shift away from the essential black subject at the ICA. He praises *Laundrette* for pushing back the boundaries of realism and giving 'expression to the complex, plural and shifting identities characteristic of contemporary British society' (p. 218). His account of the film's more formal strategies is linked to this emphasis; the section is headed 'Formal hybridity' and emphasises the mix of aesthetic conventions Frears deploys, suggesting that *My Beautiful Laundrette* is 'something of a generic hybrid' (p. 217). We can see here a process whereby the framework provided by Hall and others is used to analyse the film and thus to streamline further the possibilities of interpretation.

Hill's emphasis on reading the film through theories of cultural identity is reinforced by other accounts in more general discussions of cinema and British identity. Malik, for instance, suggests that 'Kureishi's *My Beautiful Laundrette* … had been pivotal in foregrounding … debates around British national cinema' while Higson cites it as one of a number of films in which 'self-conscious difference' marks an apparent 'shift from a British cinema of consensus to one of heterogeneity and dissent'.[45] This emphasis on cultural identity which can then be read through into a revised version of national cinema has become the dominant way of understanding *My Beautiful Laundrette* for British academics. While this has produced interesting and convincing work, it can be problematic, leading to writing in which *Laundrette* serves an exemplary function as the film that illustrates the theory. It is as if *Laundrette* is deemed to have been written out of and because of the theory and then, in a rather hermetic move, it is judged in terms of that theory. Malik illustrates what is at stake here by suggesting that 'new Black film practices … can help us make sense of notions of ethnicity, Third cinema and the diasporic experience which have been so central to critical theory in recent years, particularly in the theoretical writings of leading Black cultural critics such as Stuart Hall, Paul Gilroy, Homi Bhabha and Kobena Mercer'.[46] This appears to conceive of film-making as a route into complex and difficult theoretical work. In such a formulation, it is perhaps worth bearing in mind that the film and the theory being used to 'explain' it *both* need to be understood in relation to each other as the products of a particular context. *My Beautiful Laundrette* can no more be read as the proof of Hall's account than Hall's account can be understood as the source of the film itself.

If British writers have tended to position and explain *My Beautiful Laundrette* in a particular institutional and theoretical context, it is interesting to note that academics from other countries have used the film for rather different purposes. There is space to consider only two examples of this. An American academic, Susan Torrey Barber, provides a reading that is much more sympathetic to the entrepreneurial ambitions of Omar and Nasser, seeing the launderette as 'a little oasis' made possible by the new endorsement of enterprise and proposing that 'this "hybrid" community built on sexual diversity benefits from the Thatcherite vision of private enterprise that serves it'.[47] Barber reads the film in a much more fixed way than other critics, finding it an optimistic film in which Omar and Johnny assume 'a leadership role as entrepreneurs, bringing two diverse communities together and creating a new hybrid community made stronger by the benefits of their enterprise' (p. 235). Omar and Johnny's relationship is 'a close and potentially lasting bond ... a healthy union that bridges diverse communities' (p. 228). This account, however interesting as an example of a view from outside some rather closed British critiques, nevertheless seems to ignore the textual evidence of contradiction and irony in the film and to misunderstand the political, authorial and institutional contexts which suggest a rather more savage account of Thatcher's entrepreneurial Britain.

Timothy Corrigan situates the film rather differently in his account of, as the subtitle puts it, 'movies and culture after Vietnam'. Here, *My Beautiful Laundrette* is compared not to other British films but to films by Scorsese and Fassbinder in an argument that links cinema, postmodernism and contemporary politics. Corrigan emphasises shifting spaces and contingent alliances in the film and the way Johnny and Omar make their (temporary) business and personal alliances out of the 'material of a rapidly deteriorating culture' driven by the 'political necessity of performing according to social and economic contingencies'.[48] He suggests that the film's 'exaggerated style and the overdetermining allegory of the plot' are similarly temporary and not entirely successful attempts 'to appropriate the street, its actions and its meanings' (pp. 223–4). In the absence of a dominant centre, marginal spaces and relationships become unexpectedly crucial and, using Benjamin and Jameson as his theoretical supports, Corrigan argues that the unexpected actions and surprises that characterise the film open up potential possibilities; 'the politics of emotional surprise frees a spectator to imagine ways one *could* cross all those contending spaces and productively form cults of shared interests' (p. 225). Although both draw on postmodernist ideas, Corrigan's account thus seems more abstract than Hill's, fitting the film, perhaps, for a more international readership.

SYLLABUSES AND COURSES

One powerful way in which *My Beautiful Laundrette* continues to have a presence is in the practices of teaching; it is by now firmly embedded in courses and syllabuses, not only in Britain and not only on film study programmes. One place where we can see this happening is in the textbooks that support post-16 education in Britain. Here, the emphases that have characterised the discourses discussed above percolate into less complex versions for the next generation. Thus, in *The Media: An Introduction*, *Laundrette* features in the section on 'Race and Ethnicity' as an example of 'the "cross-over" (from art-house to mainstream) pattern' now followed by more recent films, but it is also a case study for the section on 'Hybrid identities' in the chapter on 'Nationality'.[49] In *The Television Genre Book*, the film is again an example, this time of the shift from single plays to Channel 4 films in the early eighties.[50] The absences are also replicated in the textbooks. The entry for 'Queer cinema' in *The Film Studies Dictionary*, for instance, includes *Young Soul Rebels* and *Edward II* alongside US films but does not include *Laundrette* in this or in the entry for 'queer theory'.[51] More strikingly, *My Beautiful Laundrette* features in Lez Cook's essay on 'British Cinema' in a successful film studies textbook but is not referred to in Chris Jones's essay on 'Lesbian and Gay Cinema' in the same book, which uses *Victim* (1961) and *Looking for Langston* as British case studies.[52] Indeed, *My Beautiful Laundrette* does not even make it on to his year-by-year list of films for further viewing, though *Young Soul Rebels* and two films by Jarman do.

The textbook references, as well as the whole hinterland of debate behind them, support the use of *My Beautiful Laundrette* in the class-room so that it gets on to syllabuses, course outlines and assessment assignments. Much of this work is hidden but examples show again how the film can be used for a variety of purposes. In the British secondary school system, for instance, *Laundrette* featured as a possible film for study in the British and Irish Cinema section of the A-level qualification in Film Study taken by eighteen-year-olds. For the period 2002–04, *Laundrette* was on a prescribed list of twelve films, available for 'a study of a single film's messages and values' which 'requires the detailed study of meaning and response'.[53] The list includes the British classic *The 39 Steps* (1935)[54] and *My Beautiful Laundrette* is one of three films from the 1980s, alongside its now familiar companions, *Chariots of Fire* and a Jarman film, in this case *Last of England* (1986). The emphasis on national identity which is clear in these choices also has a regional dimension which is augmented by *Laundrette*'s London setting. Other factors that influence *Laundrette*'s inclusion are indicated elsewhere in the specification when the film is offered as a possible example in the topic 'Passion and Repression' which 'looks at issues of representation in films dealing with issues of sexuality and desire in specific social contexts'. The focus film for the topic is *Brief Encounter*, another British classic, but the rubric suggests that 'gay love may be a central area of study using films such as *Victim* or *My Beautiful Laundrette*'. The inclusion of *Laundrette* in such a syllabus indicates that it has achieved a classic status in this context, one whose 'meanings and values' would repay exploration, in the rather Leavisite language of the rubric, but that it is also useful as a film that works against the more conventional, apparently heterosexual preoccupations of *Brief Encounter*.

University courses are usually less constrained than national assessment systems and, at this level, *My Beautiful Laundrette* is useful in a range of disciplines. The film appears widely on film courses giving an overview of British cinema. One such British course on 'British Cinema and National Identity' screened *Laundrette*, accompanied by readings from Hill's *British Cinema in the 1980s* and Mercer's ICA collection, in a session on 'British Cinema in the Thatcher Era' which looks at 'the economic effects of Thatcherism on the film industry … How disastrous was Tory rule for the film industry? What was the response of British film makers to the culture of individualism and Thatcherite ideology?'.[55] Such courses use *My Beautiful Laundrette* to discuss Channel 4's production situation in the context of the economy of British cinema as well as issues of national identity. Courses in English departments, however, may define the film in terms of Kureishi, using it in the context of his other work or in a more general comparative literary study; an English course taking the latter route in the USA included a section on 'Postcolonial Tensions' which set as 'primary readings: E. M. Forster's *A Passage to India*; articles by George Orwell and Salman Rushdie, the film *My Beautiful Laundrette* about Pakistanis in London'.[56] This post-colonial emphasis is a common way of contextualising and using the film. Extensive lecture notes for the use of the film on an English course on 'Colonial and Post-colonial texts' in an Australian university, for instance, emphasise identity, marginalisation and movement as ways of reading the film and suggest that the 'film's viewpoint is decentred, distributed, and contains margins and differences within itself'.[57]

But *My Beautiful Laundrette* is clearly usable for teaching in other ways. Still within the cinema/literature nexus, another Australian course, 'The idea of youth: fiction, film and youth', addressed critical and cultural theories through the 'frame of reading literary and filmic texts which participate in the ongoing renegotiation of what youth means, and its relation to the idea of "culture"'; in this course, *My Beautiful Laundrette* joins a rather different list of films for study which also include *Rebecca* (1940), *A Clockwork Orange* (1971) and *William Shakespeare's Romeo + Juliet* (1996).[58] In history courses, the film becomes evidence; a section of a US course on 'British history 1951–1997: The Return of Liberalism' put a screening of the film alongside 'oral testimonies on the winter of discontent and Thatcher's election'.[59] And a British course on Philosophy and Film put *My Beautiful Laundrette* into another context in which a session on 'Cinema, Race and Spectatorship' brings *Laundrette* and Lee's *Do the Right Thing* (1987) together on a course that uses the work of Aristotle, Kant and Marx in 'an exploration of philosophical subjects including personal identity and moral values in different films'.[60]

Sometimes this global use of the film in English-speaking education systems has rather poignant or curious consequences. What Kureishi always thought of as a London film returns to London in a different context in the 'study abroad' programmes that US universities bring to the UK.[61] But the specificity of the British Asian position rather disappears when the film is included in the bibliography of 'Asians/Asian Americans in Film and Television' produced by the Berkeley Libraries of the University of California.[62] Certainly, we cannot assume that because the film is taught on post-colonial courses endorsing difference and hybridity students will respond in anything like a uniform way. One very interesting insight into the experience of teaching *My Beautiful Laundrette* is provided by Padmaja Challakere who included the film on the world literature syllabus of a small state college in Minnesota. Challakere used the literature that has streamlined the film – Hill, Mercer, Williamson – but the student who volunteered to give the seminar presentation refused such contextualisation and indeed, drawing on a different framework provided by Christian ideology, 'would not watch the film because of its "glamorisation of sin"'. Challakere's careful (in both senses) discussion of her students' response to the film, and to their fellow student's refusal to engage with it, points us to the fact that the 'official' version of the film which makes it usable in so many different teaching contexts does not always impose itself on students' responses.[63]

REPRESENTING BRITAIN

In 1985, Stephen Frears self-deprecatingly described *My Beautiful Laundrette* as 'a film about a gay Pakistani launderette owner'.[64] He could not have foreseen that the film would not only gain an international reputation but would also serve a representative function on behalf of Britain. But it does seem clear that the film's commercial success, its cross-over status as a quirky independent that went mainstream, combined with the interweaving of the black and the gay discourses and its usefulness in teaching about how changes in British culture were experienced and conceptualised, all helped to make the film officially

usable as a representative of a rather different kind of Britain than that
envisaged by Mrs Thatcher in the 1980s. One institution that uses *My
Beautiful Laundrette* in this way is the British Council, which has a
remit that includes broadening and building up audiences for British
film abroad and providing material and speakers for seminars, master
classes and workshops on British cinema. *My Beautiful Laundrette* is
included in the Education Section's 'Ethnicity bibliography', the only
video to be listed, alongside books on post-colonialism, race relations
and identity.[65] The Film and Television Department was unable to
provide a detailed breakdown of how *My Beautiful Laundrette* had
been used in its work, but the list of places where the film had been
shown, under its auspices, in the late nineties included Turkey, Italy,
the Czech Republic, Belarus, Indonesia, Tanzania, Bangladesh, Russia
and east Jerusalem.

We get a glimpse of how the film is used in these contexts through
some examples. Thus, a large and prestigious six-month retrospective
event at the Pompidou Centre in Paris in 2000 screened *Laundrette*
along with other work by Frears, whose 1995 television celebration of
British cinema, *Typically British*, had covered the ground earlier. A more
routine example perhaps would be an event called 'Transcultural Vibes
from the UK', organised in Hamburg in 1999, at which *My Beautiful Laundrette* was among the films screened to illustrate Britain as a
multicultural society.[66] These are mainly screening opportunities, but
lectures and discussions are used, alongside films, to give information
about the British context. Such events may be developed with existing British Studies or Film Studies programmes. An example of this
would be a two-day event, 'Film as cultural representation in relation
to British studies', organised by the Department of English, University
of Szeged, hosted in March 2000 by Collegium Budapest, under the
umbrella of the British Council's British Studies project. It featured
academics from Britain and Hungary who gave papers on a range of
British films, mainly from the 1980s and 1990s. *My Beautiful Laundrette*
featured in two such papers. The first, by Sári László (University of
Pécs), 'The Intersection of Race, Class and Sexuality in Stephen Frears'
My Beautiful Laundrette or Whose Dirty Laundry Is It?', appears to
follow the academic emphasis on identity outlined above in its emphasis
on 'the discourses shaping Omar's and Johnny's story' but also looks
at narrative and 'its possible effects on viewers'. The second paper,
though, 'Using Films in Introducing English Studies', by Szőnyi György
Endre, placed the film in a rather different context, a pedagogical one

in which *Laundrette* is used with *Educating Rita* (1983) to introduce the 'key theoretical concepts of cultural studies which form the backbone' of the introduction to the British Studies course at the University of Szeged. Here, *My Beautiful Laundrette* features as a film that is helpful in 'bringing the conceptual framework closer to the students'.[67] The pervasiveness of the film in this context is confirmed by the fact that an article on this topic had previously been published in a special British cinema issue of the British Council-sponsored *Journal for the Study of British Cultures*.[68]

   This intertwining of academic study and the promotion of British film is taken a stage further in British Council support for 'A special supplement on Contemporary British Cinema' published by the American magazine *Cineaste*. The supplement was largely written by British academics, and although the emphasis was on the late nineties *My Beautiful Laundrette* is used as an example in various ways: it is a Channel 4 film for John Hill; 'the defining South London film of the late 80s' for Charlotte Brunsdon; the best-known example of eighties films which 'largely ignored their residual audience base in search of alternative, gender, multicultural and polysexual markets' for Stephen Chibnall; and one of the first 'British-Asian-themed feature films to claim a mainstream market' for Cary Rajinder Sawhney, the BFI's Project Leader for Cultural Diversity.[69] The ability of *Laundrette* to exemplify different aspects of British cinema and culture (institution, place, identity, audience) is clearly demonstrated in such passing references in this range of work.

ON THE STAGE

The reappearance of films in other forms – book or theme park, T-shirt or burger promotion – has become a commonplace for the blockbuster but is less usual for a Film on Four, beyond the translation to video or DVD. In the case of *My Beautiful Laundrette*, however, a more radical transformation took place. Snap Theatre Company took it out on the road as a touring play. Snap had done adaptations of novels and Andy Graham, the producer, chose *Laundrette* as its first film adaptation because the company wanted to attract a younger and more ethnically mixed audience. The attraction did not rely on previous knowledge of the film, which was not specifically referred to in the publicity, but on the idea that 'issues of racism, sexuality, bigotry, violence and politics' could be dealt with in a 'compassionate, humorous and hugely entertaining way'.[70] The adaptation by Andy Graham and Roger Parsley was from Kureishi's script with new music which was a 'fusion of various styles and flavours, moving from traditional ragas to the 80s scene'. The production also used video to project images and voices of, for instance, the gang members when Johnny is tempted by his old ways. In using electronic images in this way, the designers felt that they were not drawing on cinema but doing something different: 'unlike cinema, where the whole reality lies in this fleeting impression of lights, projection on stage rather tries to add another level of vision to how the story is told'. The intention was to contrast realism with music, dance and decor that drew on 'magical Bollywood glitter'.[71] In this format, then, from January to June 2002, *My Beautiful Laundrette* went on a demanding journey, visiting over forty venues in England and Wales, from big city centres to small rural communities and from London suburbs to the heart of Wales.

This theatrical production is particularly interesting in that it offers a reworking that reflects back on the original in an unusual way, a commutation test which allows us to see the film in relation to an alternative version. Two particular elements are pertinent here. The first was the decision to change the period and to shift the action from the Britain of Margaret Thatcher to that of Tony Blair. Andy Graham felt that the issues were still contemporary but that the setting had to be changed if the play was to reach young people who had no knowledge of Mrs Thatcher and for whom the 1980s were 'a frozen moment in time'.[72] The production therefore took the risk of going against one streamlined reading of the film as quintessentially a comment on British society in the 1980s, a risk that did not come off for all critics. sEarly in the tour, the *Guardian* began its broadly supportive review by specifically reminding readers that the film had been 'one of the first British films to seriously dissect the effects of Thatcherism on British society' and regarded the updating to the 'Blairite era' as 'spurious' and 'absurd'.[73] A later review by a critic who appeared not to know the film ('When the lights came up at the interval, I didn't know what would happen to our uncertain heroes') referred, however, to the success of right-wing racist parties in recent elections in Britain and France: 'the play is about Britain now and we can make it end the way we want, with the triumph of love over hatred or the other way round'.[74] In this case, the difference was not just a result of the timing of the reviews but also of how far the established critical context for the film provided a framework for understanding the play which was inescapable for some critics.

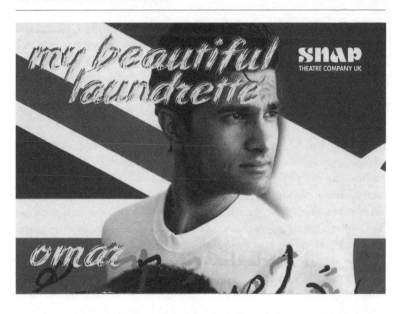

11a and b. *Publicity material for Snap Theatre Company's production of* My Beautiful Laundrette *in 2001/2, which reworked the representation of Omar and Johnny.* (Reproduced courtesy of Snap Theatre Company UK)

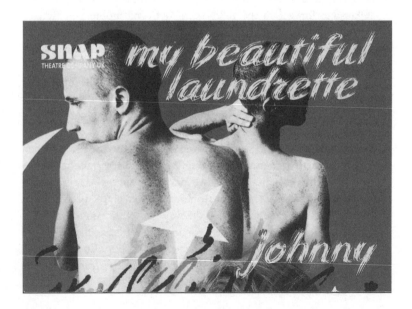

The other area the play brought into focus was that of characterisation and performance, particularly in relation to the two women
characters, Rachel and Tania, and to Johnny. The position of the two
women was given particular expression in the play in their own added
monologues which pointed up the more feminist aspects of their position, but the characterisation seemed cruder. Tanya (Catherine Mobley)
was always shown in modern dress and additional dialogue with her
father reinforced, somewhat monotonously, her aggressive contempt
for him. Rachel (Kii Kendrick), sexily dressed in red, fulfilled 'all the
predictable stereotypes of the Other Woman'[75] which Field had avoided.
She was less warm, for instance, so that her claim to know Johnny's
mother came over as something of a threat. In this contrast, one can
see how the visual use of Rachel as mediator in the film and the tenderness of Field's performance undermined some of the tendencies of the
script which were revived in this theatrical version. On the other hand,
the play restored to Johnny (Rowan Talbot) the sense of change and
conscience that Day-Lewis's star performance had tended to override.
The play began with Johnny begging for money for drugs and vow-
ing to move on. He was presented as shambling and pathetic so that
a job at the launderette made more sense as an opportunity for him.
His debates with himself and the larger-than-life projections of gang
members ('I'm fucking listening,' he tells them) gave a greater sense of
the emotional and moral shifts Johnny has to make. By contrast, Omar
(Harvinder S. Bhere) was more assertive and confident, the characterisation perhaps being changed by a different social context in 2002
in which a young and successful Asian is not such a media rarity. In
the play, then, the two actors balance each other more equally so that,
while the relationship remained narratively precarious, their presence
as a couple was more coherent.

This section has presented only a fraction of the material that has
accreted around *My Beautiful Laundrette*, but enough to show the
wide range of uses made of the film. My intention is not to argue
that its meaning changes depending on the individual viewer but that
the contexts and circumstances of viewing can position the film differently, making it undertake different kinds of work well beyond the
screen. British cinema has its share of conservative mythic films – *Brief
Encounter*, *The Blue Lamp* (1950), *The Dam Busters* (1955), *Chariots of
Fire* – which classically rework emotional restraint, doggedness and
duty into a source of national pride. *My Beautiful Laundrette* has to my

mind also achieved mythic status, but for rather different audiences. It functions as a myth for the cultural left, offering an example, rather ironically given Kureishi's position, of the acme of progessiveness, a model of what interventionist film-making in a particular institutional space on a shoestring budget might achieve; it works also as a myth of identity, offering the hope of reworking culture and self into a new, vibrant version of what it means to be British; and it works as a defiantly secular, ironic and joyous myth of the experience of being young and ambitious in a society that is going to be forced into change.

Of course, much has changed since *My Beautiful Laundrette* was made and maybe the myth is wearing thin. In July 2002, Channel 4's decision to retrench by closing down FilmFour, the ambitious late-nineties version of Film on Four, was seen by many as another blow to the British film industry. Once again, *My Beautiful Laundrette* was wheeled out as one of '12 landmark Channel 4 productions', with some suggestion of a silver lining in that Channel 4 might be 'forced back to smaller, riskier films'.[76] But the notion that less money might help the British film industry return to creativity seems disingenuous and perhaps based on a misunderstanding of the particular circumstances that made films like *Laundrette* successful. And the British Asian experience has not been magically changed by cultural transformation. The events of 11 September 2001 have put the values of multiculturalism under severe pressure and, in Britain, violence in the northern towns of Oldham, Burnley and Bradford earlier that summer was a reminder of the continuing 'confusion, anger and frustration of mainly poor, first and second generation Asians struggling to define an identity in Britain'. This quotation comes from a contribution by 'Pranjal Tiwari, UK' to a BBC news website set up to mark the start of the UN World Conference Against Racism in September 2001; it suggested '10 key moments in UK race relations' and invited additions to the list. Perhaps *My Beautiful Laundrette* still has work to do in this changed environment, for, among all the other political and sporting events suggested, one film had been added to the list by 'Darren, UK': 'The 1985 film *My Beautiful Laundrette* mattered immensely, as it expressed the nascent idea that modern, cool, Britain was essentially about multi-ethnicity. In particular, from here on there was no doubt that quality modern British art would often be about multi-ethnicity.'[77]

Notes

1. CROSSING OVER: THE MAKING OF THE FILM

1. Stuart Hall, 'New Ethnicities', *Black Film British Cinema*, ICA Document 7, London, 1989, p. 30.

2. Broadcasting Act 1981 cited in John Hill's account of the establishment of Channel 4, *British Cinema in the 1980s* (Oxford: Clarendon Press, 1999), p. 54.

3. *Sight & Sound*, 50(4), autumn 1981, p. 241.

4. 'Getting the Right Approach: Channel Four and the British Film Industry', in J. Hill and M. McLoone (eds), *Big Picture, Small Screen: The Relations between Film and Television* (Luton: John Libbey Media/University of Luton Press, 1996), p. 178.

5. Hill, *British Cinema in the 1980s*, p. 59.

6. John Pym, *Film on Four: A Survey 1982–1991* (London: BFI, 1992), p. 8.

7. *Screen Digest Dossier* (London: BFI, 1990), p. 6 .

8. Simon Perry, 'Cannes, Festivals and the Movie Business', *Sight & Sound*, 50 (4), autumn 1981, p. 231.

9. *Sight & Sound*, 53 (2), spring 1984, p. 115. Subsequent quotations are taken from the same source unless indicated.

10. *Sight & Sound*, 54 (1), winter 1984/5, p. 10.

11. Perry, 'Cannes, Festivals and the Movie Business', p. 231.

12. See Robert Murphy, 'The Public Has a Brain', *Sight & Sound*, 53 (1), winter 1983/4, pp. 8–11 for a discussion of these problems.

13. Quoted in Duncan Petrie, *Creativity and Constraint in the British Film Industry* (London: Macmillan, 1991), p. 105.

14. *Screen International*, no. 524, 23 November 1985, pp. 82 and 84. Kureishi refers elsewhere to writing the script in Pakistan in February 1985 but it would appear to have been a year earlier. 'Introduction', *My Beautiful Laundrette and the Rainbow Sign* (London: Faber & Faber, 1986), p. 41.

15. *Interview*, April 1987, p. 92.

16. Lester Friedman and Scott Stewart, 'Keeping His Own Voice: An Interview with Stephen Frears', in W. W. Dixon (ed.), *Re-viewing British Cinema 1900–1992* (New York: State University of New York Press, 1994), p. 224.

17. James Saynor, 'Sheer Frears', *Stills*, November 1985, pp. 11–12.

18. See Bart Moore-Gilbert, *Hanif Kureishi* (Manchester: Manchester University Press, 2001) for an account of Kureishi's theatrical work.

19. *Screen International*, no. 524, 23 November 1985, p. 84.

20. Hanif Kureishi, 'Dirty Washing', *Time Out*, no. 795, 14 November 1985, p. 25.

21. Kureishi, 'Introduction', p. 41.

22. Kureishi, 'Dirty Washing', p. 26.

23. Hanif Kureishi, 'Scenes from a Marriage', *Monthly Film Bulletin*, 52.622, November 1985, p. 333; *Guardian*, 14 November 1985.

24. Kureishi, 'Introduction', pp. 43 and 44.

25. Kureishi, 'Dirty Washing', p. 26.

26. 39th Edinburgh International Film Festival programme, 10–25 August 1985, p. 33.

27. *Financial Times*, 23 August 1985, p. 11.

28. *Guardian*, 22 August 1985, p. 11.

29. *Monthly Film Bulletin*, 52.622, p. 333; *Sunday Times*, 25 August 1985, p. 33.

30. *Guardian*, 22 August 1985, p. 11.

31. *Screen International*, no. 524, p. 84; Kureishi, 'Dirty Washing', p. 26; and 'Introduction', p. 6.

32. David Robinson commented on the fact that, at the film's 'startling appearance' at Edinburgh, 'Kureishi's script tended to get most of the credit'. *Sight & Sound*, 55 (1), winter 1985/6, p. 67.

33. *Monthly Film Bulletin*, 52.622, p. 333 (my emphasis).

34. During the early 1980s, the GLC, as the body responsible for elements of London's local government, consistently opposed the Thatcher government. It tried to bring together groups excluded on the grounds of race and sexuality as well as class and often caused controversy by using culture as an arena for struggle. It was finally abolished in March 1986.

35. *Screen International*, no. 526, 7 December 1985, p. 40.

36. *New Statesman*, 15 November 1985.

37. *Mail on Sunday*, 17 November 1985.

38. *Screen International*'s figures at this time were based on a restricted number of cinemas and did not include some independent repertory and second-run screens, though these were sometimes the subject of a separate report.

39. *Screen International*, no. 541, 29 March 1986, p. 37.

40. *Variety*, 24 February 1986.

41. *New York Times*, 7 March 1986; *Cineaste*, xv (1), 1986, p. 39.

42. *Guardian*, 6 May 1986.

43. Pauline Kael, 'The Current Cinema Yes Yes', *New Yorker*, 10 March 1986, p. 117.

44. Vincent Canby, *New York Times*, 7 March 1986.

45. Richard Corliss, *Time*, 17 March 1986.

46. Pym, *Film on Four*, p. 64.

47. June Givanni, 'In Circulation: Black Films in Britain', *Black Film British Cinema*, p. 40.

48. Mercer, 'Recoding Narratives of Race and Nation', in ibid., p. 4.

49. Colin McCabe, 'Black Film in 80s Britain', in ibid., p. 52.

50. 'Review', *Sight & Sound*, 52 (1), winter 1982/3, p. 70.

51. Judith Williamson, 'Two Kinds of Otherness: Black Film and the Avant-garde', *Black Film British Cinema*, p. 36. The academic journal *Screen* was strongly associated with theoretical work on film which used complex language to explore psychoanalytic and ideological concepts.

52. *Spectator*, 23 November 1985, p. 42.

53. *Screen International*, no. 493, 20 April 1985, p. 64.

54. Film Festival programme, p. 33.

55. *Observer*, 25 August 1985; *Glasgow Herald*, 22 August 1985.

56. *Sunday Times*, 25 August 1985.

57. *Scotsman*, 19 August 1985.

58. *Times Educational Supplement*, 30 August 1985.

59. *Girl about Town*, 18 November 1985; *Spare Rib*, February 1986, p. 32.

60. Cited in Julian Henriques, 'Realism and the New Language', originally in *Artrage*, 13, summer 1986, reprinted in *Black Film British Cinema*, p. 19.

61. Mahmood Jamal, 'Dirty Linen', reprinted in *Black Film British Cinema*, p. 21.

62. Perminder Dhillon-Kashyap, 'Locating the Asian Experience', *Screen*, 29 (4), autumn 1988, p. 125.

63. Sarita Malik, 'Beyond "a Cinema of Duty"? The Pleasures of Hybridity: Black British Film of the 1980s and 1990s', in A. Higson (ed.), *Dissolving Views. New Writings on British Cinema* (London: Cassell, 1998), p. 209.

64. Kureishi, 'Dirty Washing', p. 26.

65. Kureishi, 'Scenes from a Marriage', p. 333.

66. Henriques, 'Realism and the New Language', p. 19.

67. Mercer, 'Recoding Narratives', p. 11.

68. Mercer, 'Black Art and the Burden of Representation', in *Welcome to the Jungle* (London: Routledge, 1994), p. 235.

69. Henriques, 'Realism and the New Language', p. 19.

70. Frears himself identified crossing over as one of the themes of the film but in a more fixed way. Referring to a shot in which Omar gets out of the car and walks over to Johnny (which does not appear very clearly in the film), Frears commented, 'Here I realized that someone was crossing over from alienation to being white … It's about a journey from one side to another. So I realized the shot that arrived quite intuitively perfectly expressed what

the film was doing, what the film was about; crossing over and integration through separation' ('Keeping His Own Voice', p. 226). A reading that relies on Omar leaving his family to become white does not actually seem to me to be evidenced by the film, but the point here is that the version of crossing over offered by black cultural critics was more generous and flexible; it enabled the film to fit a context that Frears's version would not.

71. Hall, 'New Ethnicities', p. 30.

72. *Guardian*, 22 August 1985.

73. David Docherty, Michael Tracy and David Morrison, *Keeping Faith. Channel 4 and Its Audience* (London: John Libbey/Broadcasting Research Unit, 1988), p. 29.

74. Kureishi, 'Dirty Washing', p. 26.

75. Kureishi, 'Scenes from a Marriage', p. 333.

76. *Observer*, 25 August 1985; *Monthly Film Bulletin*, 52.622, p. 333.

77. *The Listener*, 21 November 1985, p. 41; *Cineaste*, xv (1), 1986, p. 39.

78. *Gay Times*, no. 88, December/January 1986, p. 65.

79. Mark Finch, 'Victim Victorious?', *City Limits*, no. 215, 15 November 1985, p. 13.

80. Hall, 'New Ethnicities', p. 27.

81. Mercer, 'Recoding Narratives', p. 12.

82. Hall, 'New Ethnicities', p. 29.

83. Barbara Klinger, *Melodrama and Meaning. History, Culture and the Films of Douglas Sirk* (Bloomington: Indiana University Press, 1994), p. 27.

2. TRANSFORMATIONS: FILM ANALYSIS

1. Tzvetvan Todorov, *The Poetics of Prose* (Ithaca, NY: Cornell University Press, 1977), p. 135.

2. The dialogue quoted is taken from the film, which differs at points from the published script.

3. Hans Zimmer, who worked with Stanley Myers on the music, is an innovator in the use of computer-synthesised soundtracks and the integration of electronic and traditional orchestral music.

4. Janice Radway, *Reading the Romance. Women, Patriarchy and Popular Literature* (Chapel Hill: University of North Carolina Press, 1984); Thomas Schatz, *Hollywood Genres: Formulas, Filmmaking and the Studio System* (New York: Random House, 1981).

5. *Sight & Sound*, 54 (1), winter 1984/5, p. 10.

6. Frears uses the device of interlocking spaces elsewhere. The music shop in *High Fidelity* (2000) has an internal office but it is used to much less complex effect.

7. John Caughie, *Television Drama* (Oxford: Oxford University Press, 2000), p. 145.

8. 'The Social Art Cinema: A Moment in the History of British Film and Television Culture', in C. Williams (ed.), *Cinema: The Beginnings and the Future* (London: University of Westminster Press, 1996).

9. *Sight & Sound*, 50 (4), 1981, p. 119.

10. Hill, *British Cinema in the 1980s*, p. 81. The 'heritage film' is the term given to a group of British films of classic novels which emerged in the 1980s. Their emphasis on period costume, beautiful landscapes and the upper classes seemed to indicate a nostalgia for the days of empire, though critical debate on the pleasures they offer continues.

11. Frears, in 'Keeping His Own Voice', p. 232.

12. Kureishi, 'Dirty Washing', p. 25.

13. *Sunday Telegraph*, 17 November 1985.

14. *Western Mail*, 18 January 1986; *Guardian*, 14 November 1985.

15. *Spectator*, 23 November 1985, p. 41.

16. *New Socialist*, January 1986, p. 24; *The Listener*, 21 November 1985, p. 41.

17. *Sunday Mirror*, 17 November 1985.

18. *Sunday Times*, 17 November 1985.

19. *Variety*, 21 August 1985, p. 122.

20. Ibid., 18 March 1986, p. 59.

21. *Village Voice*, 18 March 1986; *New York Times*, 7 March 1986.

22. Kael, 'The Current Cinema', p. 119.

23. *Sunday Times Magazine*, 24 November 1985; *Gay Times*, no. 88, p. 47; *What's On*, 14 November 1985.

24. London *Standard*, 22 November 1985.

25. *Sunday Times Magazine*, 24 November 1985.

26. *What's On*, 14 November 1985; *Guardian*, 31 May 1986.

27. Joan Julie Buck, 'Actor from the Shadows', *New Yorker*, 12 October 1992, p. 51.

28. *Sunday Times Magazine*, 24 November 1985, p. 84.

29. *New York Times*, 21 March 1986; Sarris, *Village Voice*. This praise continued as the film toured the USA. Roger Ebert commented that the two performances were 'an affirmation of the miracle of acting: that one man could play these two opposites is astonishing' (*Chicago Sun-Times*, 4 November 1986).

30. Kael, 'The Current Cinema', p. 119.

31. *Guardian*, 31 May 1986.

32. Frears, in 'Keeping His Own Voice', p. 238.

33. *Trikone*, July 2002; *Empire*, no. 58, April 1994, p. 38.

34. *Eastern Eye*, 15 August 1995.

35. *Guardian*, 14 February 1987.
36. Ibid.
37. *Spare Rib*, May 1991, p. 32; *Daily Mirror*, 10 August 1990.
38. *Daily Mail*, 2 August 1990.
39. Alison Donnell (ed.), *Companion to Contemporary Black British Culture* (London: Routledge, 2002), p. 325.
40. *Daily Express*, 25 June 1965.
41. *Daily Mail*, 10 May 1980.
42. *Sunday Telegraph*, 10 November 1985.
43. *Daily Mail*, 13 January 1986.
44. Ibid., 21 January 1987.
45. *Guardian*, 13 November 1985.
46. Richard Dyer, 'Feeling English', *Sight & Sound*, 4 (3) March 1994, pp. 16–19.
47. *Sunday Express*, 12 March 1989.
48. Kureishi, 'Dirty Washing', pp. 25, 26.
49. Commenting on a later theatrical performance, *Eastern Eye* (18 April 1997) suggested that he was the only one in an Asian cast who avoided 'that infuriating Peter Sellers caricature, desperate to please a White audience'.
50. *Gay Times*, no. 88, p. 49.
51. *Daily Mail*, 13 January 1986.
52. *Eastern Eye*, 5 January 1996.
53. *The Times*, 27 November 1998 .
54. *Eastern Eye*, 18 April 1997.

3. CONTINUATIONS: *LAUNDRETTE*'S REPUTATION

1. It was a featured film in May 2002 in Bravo TV schedules, for instance, and screened at the 21st Annual Political Film Festival at Richard Stockton College of New Jersey in April 2002.
2. 'Black and White in Television', in J. Givanni (ed.), *Remote Control Dilemmas of Black Intervention in British Film and TV* (London: BFI, 1995), p. 15.
3. 'Intervention for What? Black TV and the Impossibility of Politics', in ibid., p. 29.
4. 'Black, British Cinema in the Nineties: Going, Going, Gone', in R. Murphy (ed.), *British Cinema of the Nineties* (London: BFI, 2000), p. 113.
5. Jim Pines, 'British Cinema and Black Representation', in R. Murphy (ed.), *The British Cinema Book* (London: BFI, 2001), p. 182.
6. Sarita Malik, *Representing Black Britain: Black and Asian Images on Television* (London: Sage, 2002), p. 171.

7. Quoted in Stephen Bourne, *Black in the British Frame* (London, Continuum, 2001), p. 162.

8. Isaac Julien and Colin McCabe, *Diary of a Young Soul Rebel* (London: BFI, 1991), p. 116.

9. Malik, 'Beyond "a Cinema of Duty"?', p. 214.

10. *Eastern Eye*, 11 February 2000.

11. *Time Out*, 3 November 1999.

12. *Independent on Sunday*, 'Culture', 10 October 1999.

13. Ibid.

14. Leslee Udwin quoted in *Evening Standard*, 2 November 1999; Director of Distribution at FilmFour quoted in *Guardian*, 10 December 1999.

15. *Evening Standard*, 2 November 1999.

16. *Detroit News*, 28 April 2000.

17. Parminder Vir, 'From Bollywood to Britain', unpublished paper delivered at BAFTA event, 4 December 2001, p. 6.

18. *East is East* actress Archie Panjabi in *The Times Magazine*, 30 October 1999. At this point the term 'Indian' is used generically even in relation to *My Beautiful Laundrette* and *East is East*, which feature Pakistani families.

19. 'Black, British Cinema in the Nineties', p. 112.

20. Gurinder Chada, 'Call That a Melting Pot?', *Guardian*, 11 April 2002.

21. *Sight & Sound*, 12 (5), May 2002, p. 39.

22. Chada, 'Call That a Melting Pot?'.

23. Vir, 'From Bollywood to Britain', p. 1.

24. *Asian Age*, 23 November 1999.

25. Sukhdev Sandhu, 'Paradise Syndrome', *London Review of Books*, 18 May 2000, p. 32.

26. See Michael O'Pray, '"New Romanticism" and the British Avant-garde Film in the Early 80s', in *The British Cinema Book*; and Stella Bruzzi, 'Two Sisters, the Fogey, the Priest and His Lover: Sexual Plurality in 1990s British Cinema', in J. Ashby and A. Higson (eds), *British Cinema of the 90s* (London: Routledge, 2000).

27. Claire Jackson and Peter Tapps (eds), *The Bent Lens World Guide to Gay and Lesbian Film* (St Kilda, Victoria: Australian Catalogue Co., 1997), p. 10.

28. Bad Object-Choices Collective (eds), *How Do I Look? Queer Film and Video* (Seattle: Bay Press, 1991); Paul Burston, 'End of the Road', in *What Are You Looking At? Queer Sex, Style and Cinema* (London: Cassell, 1995), p. 138; Ellis Hansen (ed.), *Out Takes. Essays on Queer Theory* (Durham, NC: Duke University Press, 1999).

29. Raymond Murray (ed.), *Images in the Dark* (Philadelphia, PA: TLA Publications, 1998), p. 288; Alexander Doty, *Making It Perfectly Queer. Interpreting Mass Culture* (Minneapolis: University of Minnesota Press, 1993), p. 15.

30. 'When Difference is (More Than) Skin Deep', in M. Gever, P. Parmar and J. Greyson (eds), *Queer Looks. Perspectives on Lesbian and Gay Film and Video* (London: Routledge, 1993), p. 337.

31. Thomas Waugh, 'The Third Body: Patterns in the Construction of the Subject in Gay, Male Narratives', in ibid., p. 157.

32. 'Tracing Desires: Sexuality and Media Texts', in A. Briggs and P. Cobley, *The Media. An Introduction* (Harlow: Addison, Wesley, Longman, 1998), p. 291. I am grateful to Andy Medhurst, more generally, for very valuable insights which have informed this section.

33. Alexander Doty, *Flaming Classics. Queering the Film Canon* (London: Routledge, 2000), p. 1.

34. Richard Dyer, *The Culture of Queers* (London; Routledge, 2002), p. 4.

35. Gever et al. (eds), *Queer Looks*, p. xiv.

36. Jenni Olson (ed.), *The Ultimate Guide to Lesbian and Gay Film and Video* (New York: Serpent's Tail), p. 166; Keith Howes, *Broadcasting It. An Encyclopaedia of Homosexuality on Film, Radio and TV in the UK 1923–93* (London: Cassell, 1993), p. 532.

37. Jackson and Tapps (eds), *The Bent Lens*, p. 224; Murray (ed.), *Images in the Dark*, p. 288.

38. <canoe.ca/Valentine'sDay/movies> (4 April 2002).

39. This link was noted by distributors who re-released *Laundrette* in a double bill with this later British film.

40. Review by 'Julian South' at <amazon/com/exec/obidos> (30 July 2002). In the synopsis for the DVD, Amazon updated the film more radically than usual by claiming that the launderette is transformed 'into a veritable palace, with space invaders and video screens'.

41. <chuckgriffith.com/short_take_8> (30 July 2002).

42. Christopher Williams, 'The Social Art Cinema', in Williams (ed.), *Cinema*, p. 197.

43. Caughie, *Television Drama*, p. 183.

44. Hill, *British Cinema in the 1980s*, p. xiii.

45. Malik, *Representing Black Britain*, p. 164; 'The Instability of the National', in *British Cinema Past and Present*, p. 38.

46. Malik, 'Beyond "a Cinema of Duty?"', p. 211.

47. 'Insurmountable Difficulties and Moments of Ecstasy: Ethnic and Sexual Barriers in the Films of Stephen Frears', in L. Friedman (ed.) *British Cinema and Thatcherism* (Minneapolis: University of Minnesota Press, 1993), pp. 220, 227.

48. Timothy Corrigan, *A Cinema Without Walls* (London: Routledge, 1992), p. 222.

49. Sarita Malik, 'The Construction of Black and Asian Ethnicities in British Film and Television', in Briggs and Cobley (eds), *The Media*, p. 318; Andrew Higson, 'National Identity and the Media', pp. 356–7.

50. Glen Creeber (ed.), *The Television Genre Book* (London: BFI, 2001), p. 13.

51. Steve Blandford, Barry Keith Grant and Jim Hillier (eds), *The Film Studies Dictionary* (London: Arnold, 2001), pp. 191–2.

52. Jill Nelmes (ed.), *An Introduction to Film Studies* (London: Routledge, 1999).

53. Specification 420, General Certificate of Education from Welsh Joint Education Committee, Advanced-Subsidiary, 2003, p. 18. I am very grateful to Roy Stafford for discussing this area with me.

54. This film is also featured in the British Film Guides. See Mark Glancy, *The 39 Steps* (London: I.B. Tauris, 2003).

55. <cf.ac.uk/jomec/ugd/modules> (30 July 2002).

56. <upenn.edu/Complit/undergrad/ugfall96> (30 July 2002).

57. <arts.usyd.edu.au/departs/english/1010Colonial (30 July 2002).

58. <adelaide.edu.au/English/iyouth> (7 April 2002).

59. <history.berkeley.edu/faculty/Vernon/History151B> (30 July 2002).

60. <city.ac.uk/conted/filmphi> (30 July 2002).

61. Michigan, New York and Syracuse Universities included the film on such programmes in 2002.

62. <lib.berkeley.edu/MRC/imagesasiansbib> (30 July 2002).

63. 'Fears of a Happy Ending: Homosexuality and Hanif Kureishi's *My Beautiful Laundrette* in the World Literature Classroom', in *2001 Proceedings, Annual Red River Conference on World Literature* (North Dakota State University), vol. 3, 2001, <ndsu.nodak.edu> (7 April 2002).

64. Frears, 'Sheer Frears', p. 12.

65. <britishcouncil.org> (30 July 2002).

66. <britcoun.de/d/arts/pubs/vibes99/vibes6> (30 July 2002).

67. <toddswift.com/bond> (30 July 2002).

68. Rainer Schüren, 'Teaching Different Cultures through Film. *Educating Rita* and *My Beautiful Laundrette*', in Peter Drexler (ed.), *British Cinema*, vol. 5, no. 2, 1998.

69. Cineaste, XXVI (4), fall 2001, 'Contemporary British Cinema'; 'London Films', p. 46; 'Britain's Funk Soul Brothers', p. 38; '"Another Kind of British"', p. 58.

70. Events brochure, January–March 2002, the Old Town Hall, Dacorum Borough Council, p. 8.

71. Quotations all from Snap Theatre Company programme for *My Beautiful Laundrette*. I am very grateful to Andy Graham for taking the time to discuss the production with me.

72. Review by 'Harvey O'Brien MA' at <indigo.ie/~obrienh/mbl> (30 July 2002).

73. Lyn Gardner, *Guardian*, 29 January 2002.

74. <theatre-in-wales.co.uk/reviews/index>. Review by 'Rebecca Nesvet', 4 May 2002 (30 July 2002).

75. Ibid.

76. Andrew Pulver, 'End of an Era', *Guardian*, 12 July 2002.

77. <news.bbc.co.uk/hi/english/uk/newsid> (30 July 2002).